# THREE BROTHERS - 1626

*The Ancestry of the World up to*
*1626 and Beyond to Our Day*

Stephen Hanks

For more information about this title or to order other books
and/or electronic media, contact the publisher:

Stephen Hanks
stevestarservices@yahoo.com
facebook.com/Portland Pioneers of Color Tours

ISBN:
978-1-7366786-0-2 (Paperback)
978-1-7366786-1-9 (eBook)

Printed in the United States of America

Cover and Interior design:
Van-garde Imagery • van-garde.com

# Contents

# CHAPTER ONE

# An Ancient Legend

A CATASTROPHIC STORM. FEW SURVIVORS. Three brothers. In time, their wives would bear many children, who would become the nations of the world.

A verse in the writings of the Qur'an says that those who believe and do good works will enter Gardens underneath which rivers flow to dwell forever. The writings of another holy book mentions also about gardens, rivers, and living forever:

> *"...the tree of life in the middle of the garden...there was a river flowing out of Eden to water the garden, and from there it divided into four rivers."*

This ancient story, in a book titled *Beresthith* found in the Hebrew Penteutuch, tells its version of the birth of mankind. According to the account passed down to Moses from his forefathers, the mitochondrial Eve and her husband Adam, the first modern humans, raised sons and daughters, including the legendary Cain and Abel. However, through their third son Seth sprang the great ship-builder Noah and his sons – *Three Brothers* - who along with their wives were told by God to build an ark to preserve the human race from a great catastrophic storm that has never occurred again on this earth according to recorded history.

There are just as many people today who do not accept that story as fact, as there are those who do. It is extremely amazing that three major religions of the world – Judaism, Christianity, Islam – record an account of three brothers named Shem, Ham, and Japheth had a father named Noah and built an ark because of an impending rainstorm that deluged the earth. Whether some believe or not, it is a fascinating fact that there are hundreds of legends worldwide in various languages and cultures of an ancient world of people destroyed by water, but for a few survivors on a mountain. We will mention some of these legends shortly. But for now, let us paraphrase the rest of the biblical account for those who have not heard it: 'the Ark was completed. Noah's family entered inside. God closed the door. It began raining. The rain continued. The rain wouldn't stop, until after 150 days. After one year, three brothers emerged from the vessel – Shem, Ham, and Japheth, whose lineages bore all the nations and families of the world.'

A word for the skeptics – Suppose if these three brothers really did exist, would there be historical evidence of them and their descendants? If we could trace the genealogy of these brothers and their pedigree to the nations of the world up to our day, what would the record reveal? What would history show? And what could it say, if anything, about our future on this planet as a human race?

In the following attempts to answer these questions, using factual writings and historical legends as support, let us begin by revisiting the legend of the "Paradise of God" in the utopian "Garden of Eden." In the book Berethith, Moses continues, stating that the river flowing out of Eden split into four rivers:

> "The name of the first river is Pishon, encircling the entire land
> of Havilah where there is gold…The name of the second river is

*Gihon, encircling the entire land of Cush. The name of the third river is Hiddekel, going to the east of Assyria. And the fourth river is the Euphrates."*

Modern researchers have yet to identify the first two rivers mentioned, the Pishon and Gihon. However, much evidence has been written throughout history identifying the other two. The Hiddekel River was known in Persian as the Tigra, or in Greek as the Tigris, which has its source in Central Armenia. Its western headstream is a few miles from the source of the Euphrates River, which also is Armenia. One of the popular traditional foods of Armenia is *Harissa*, a thick porridge made up of roasted wheat and lamb or chicken. Another local dish is grilled barbeque skewers called *shish* and *shampoors*, made up of marinated pork ribs and seasoned with salt and pepper. Being that these two rivers flow so close to each other, it is very possible that these two rivers could easily have had a single source at one time thousands of years ago. The Euphrates has two sources. One is at Kara Su, in the SE corner of the Black Sea. The other source is Murat Nehri, originating between Lake Van and Mount Ararat. These two sources unite near the city of Keban. We will examine more closely what else Moses wrote about these rivers shortly.

Now let's examine any evidence of a "shipbuilder" named Noah, who, according to the Hebrew legend of popular belief built along with his wife, three sons, and their wives a large floating vessel made of cedar wood timbers and pitch tar to save the human race. It is estimated that over 500 flood legends have been told by more than 250 tribes and peoples. For example, in Greek mythology Zeus, the king of the Olympian gods, decided to destroy rebellious mankind by a deluge. To survive the coming waters, Deucalion the king of Phthia constructed an ark, carried his wife Pyrrha and provisions onboard;

Greece was flooded, and the mountains of Thessaly were formed due to the tremendous rainfall; The ark rested on Moumt Parmassus in Thessaly; Deucalion offered a sacrifice to Zeus, who commanded Decalion and Pyrrha to throw stones behind them; Those thrown by Deucalion became men, while those thrown by Pyrrha became women.

Another flood legend comes from Siberia, Russia, which held that a giant frog supporting the earth moved, causing the globe to be flooded, but an old man and his family survived on a raft that landed on a high mountain. And many have heard of the Babylonian Epic of Gilamesh, who had been told to build a ship and bring his family and animals inside it to survive a flood; The ship went aground on a mountain, and the family made an animal sacrifice to their god in thankfulness. These, and many other such legends of a flood, are found all over the world. More of these examples will be mentioned later.

The Greek Septuagint of the Hebrew Testament marks the account of a global flood during the third millennium in the year 2370 BCE According to the chronicle passed down to Moses, the Egyptian-raised Hebrew leader and great-grandson of Levi, the ship vessel that Shem, Ham, and Japheth helped their father Noah to build ended up on the mountains of Ararat. The Ararat mountains are today located in Armenia.

As the waters receded and the dry land appeared, as one could imagine, the eight survivors exited from the water-caulked vessel and the three brothers soon made their way down the mountainous range to begin their life anew.

In time, their wives would bear many children. Shem and his wife and children no doubt took the task of choosing a region of land in which to raise his progeny. His brother Japheth and wife and family also sought a roomy land boundary for their offspring to thrive.

Their brother Ham and his wife and seed would also choose a spacious land area to raise his many sons. We recall that Moses spoke of *the entire land of Cush* which was encircled by a river called Gihon. Ham had a son named Cush. So Ham and his family lived at one time, it appears, by the Black Sea near the present-day countries of Georgia and Armenia. But, was Moses perhaps referring instead to the Nubian Ethiopic Kingdom of "Kush" that rose to power in world history? No, because that kingdom had not yet rose to power to sit on the throne of Pharoah in Egypt at the time Moses wrote his account in 1513 BCE.

Therefore, Moses was referring to an earlier *Land of Cush* that was either still in existence in his day, or in the memory of the older generation who were still alive during the time Moses recorded his words. The older generation Hebrews, held as slaves for decades under Pharoah, knew the story about the Land of Cush and passed down the knowledge of its existence to Moses. Is there any evidence today that such a land did exist? We will revisit this question again in Chapters Two and Three, where we will discuss the discovery of a Black Hamitic village still inhabited today in the present Republic of Georgia.

Let us first examine the beginning lineages of brothers Japheth and Shem.

# CHAPTER TWO

# The Sons of Japheth and Shem

**The sons of Japheth, (according to Biblical writings), were Gomer, Magog, Madai, Javan, Tubal, Meshech, and Tiras. From these names sprang European tribes.**

BEFORE WE EMBARK ON OUR journey in this discussion, let us say at the outset that today, many, many people define themselves as multi-racial – meaning they ascribe to more than one ancestry or ethnicity. We will examine the genetics of this later, but for now, let us start with a basic overview of the sons of Japheth. For those who identify with European ancestry, let us revisit the history of world civilization – from the beginning. And as we do, please do not be shocked by what we are about to learn.

According to the historian Flavius Josephus, Japheth's son Magog was related to the East Iranian Scythians, a nomadic people of Iranian origin in the land of Scythia, a region in Central Asia. Scythia stretched from the Caspian Sea in the west, to China and Mongolia in the east, and from Afghanistan and Iran in the south. The ancient Greeks gave the name Scythia to all the lands north-east of Europe and the northern coast of the Black Sea, in what is modern-day Ukraine and southern Russia.

Japheth's son Madai was a progenitor of the Medes, part of the Medo-Persian dual empire. The Medes and the Persians were related

peoples of Aryan tribes. The earliest evidence of a Caucasian civilization is found in the plains of Armenian Uratu (Ararat). That ancient
region would today be large parts of modern Armenia, Azerbaijan,
Georgia, and parts of Iran and Turkey. The early inhabitants built
mud-brick dwellings with rooms. Farming and breeding livestock
was their economical base. They also had developed the skills of
Metallurgy. Their metal goods were distributed to areas now known
today as Anatolia, Syria, and Palestine.

There are millions of people today who identify with Jewish and
Arabic-speaking cultures. Let us now turn our attention to the sons
of Shem. We will explore the sons of Ham soon.

**The sons of Shem (according to ancient Hebrew writings
and tradition) were Arpachshad, Elam, Asshur, Lud, and
Aram.**

According to the Greek Septuagint, the meticulous genealogy of
the Hebrew Jews pointed to the year 2370 BCE in the third millennium as the precise time of a great global deluge that Shem, Ham,
and Japheth eye-witnessed as survivors. The three brothers would
emerge out of the ark container in the highlands of Armenia and,
after pitching camp there for some period of time, began their migration "eastward" through Anatolia toward Shinar in Mesopotamia.

Anatolia, the large peninsula in modern-day Turkey, was called
the "Land of the Hatti", according to cuneiform tablets belonging to
the Akkadian Empire (2350 – 2150 BCE), who were descendants of
Japheth's brother Ham. But the peninsula of Anatolia was called by the
Greeks *Asia*. After the three brothers and their families had explored
Shinar, a serious breach of peaceful co-existence occurred between one
of Ham's sons and one of Shem's sons. How did this take place?

Ham had five sons (See Chapter Three). One of them, Nimrod,

founded the kingdom of Akkad. Shem's son Asshur was the ancestor of the Kingdom of Assyria. Around the 24th century BCE, Nimrod's kingdom of Akkad made an act of aggression against his first cousin Asshur, and his kingdom Assyria, in modern-day Iraq. The Babylonian Talmud recorded the following text:

> *"Why, then, was he called Nimrod? Because he stirred up the whole world to rebel against the sovereignty of God."*

Nimrod, whose name meant "Rebel" in Hebrew, lived up to his reputation as a mighty hunter, not only in pursuing animal game, but also in human flesh, as he waged military campaigns against his cousins and his father's relatives. He continued his military expansion, founding other kingdoms such as well-known Ninevah and Babylon. According to the Hebrew Pentuetuch, Nimrod's building project was divinely halted by supernatural means. While building the famed tower of Babel, a bold tower project slated to be the tallest religious structure of its day, the workers all suddenly became confused in how to carry out the engineering feat, as each man was mysteriously unable to communicate with the other. Moses in effect was saying: God has confused your language into many languages." Interestingly, Shem's firstborn son Arpachshad had a great-grandson named "Peleg" (2269 – 2030 BCE) whose name meant "Division", *"for in his days the earth was divided,"* Moses stated. The world at that time was indeed divided.

But Asshur's kingdom did not remain defenseless forever. As history showed, Assyria became a military power to the degree of Babylon and Akkad. In time, Assyria became known for its sadistic torture of captured enemies in warfare. However, despite Assyria and Babylon maintaining a close relationship as neighboring allies, Babylon eventually turned against their ally Assyria and conquered them in the year 632 BCE.

Now let us focus more on the offspring of Japheth. During the 13th century BCE along the Black Sea coast arose a number of tribes which formed the *Kingdom of Colchis*. Tribes such as the Mossynocci, the Macrones, and the Tubareni were located in present-day western Georgia. The Kingdom of Colchis is remembered in the mythological stories of Jason and the Argonauts and the Golden Fleece. Historian Herodotus stated that he believed the Colchians were an ancient Egyptian race:

"For it is plain to see that the Colchians are Egyptians; and what I say, I myself noted before I heard it from others. When it occurred to me, I inquired of both peoples; and the Colchians remembered the Egyptians better than the Egyptians remembered the Colchians; the Egyptians said that they considered the Colchians part of Sesostris' army. I myself guessed it, partly because they are dark-skinned and wooly-haired; though that indeed counts for nothing, since other peoples are, too; but my better proof was that the Colchians and Egyptians and Ethiopians are the only nations that have from the first practiced circumcision."

This was also said about the tribes of Colchis along the Black Sea – So completely different in language and appearance from other Indo-European nations in the region, that ancient historians had various theories trying to explain away their origins. Pliny the Elder said of them:

"The Colchians were governed by their own kings in the earliest ages, that Seostris king of Egypt was overcome in Scythia, and put to fight, by the king of Colchis, which if true, that the Colchins not only had kings in those times, but were a very powerful people."

Modern-day historians are still trying to understand the ancient Colchis tribes. There is a city today once roamed by the Colchians – the city of Abkhazia, where live an ethnic group known as the

Caucasian Africans. They are also called the Abkhazians of African descent. Who are they? A newspaper called *The Afro-American* wrote an article in 1973 about whether Africans were living in the Soviet Union. The reporter traveled to the Caucasus mountain region on the east coast of the Black Sea, to a city called Abkhazia, then in the Soviet Republic of Georgia. The reporter reached Sukhumi, the capital city of Abkhazia, and while there discovered dark-skinned people of African descent living in the city, but dressed Russian and speaking Abkhazian. The cuisine of this region includes boiled or roasted meat and chicken along with *mamalyga* (corn meal) vegetables, walnuts, and served with spicy sauces flavored with *Ajika* (red pepper, garlic, and herbs), and a bottle of *Anakopia* white wine, *Apsny* sweet red wine, or vodka. This was not, however, the first time the subject had been reported on. Over one hundred years ago, in the early 1900's, several researchers had attempted to answer the phenomenon of the Caucasian Africans and their origin. Many concluded they were descendants of former African slaves who were brought to Russia during the 16th century CE. But is this the only explanation? We will examine this question further in Chapter Three.

The Hispani, also known as the *Iberians*, descending from Japheth's grandson Tarshish, were a population of people inhabiting alongside the Colchis region. The Iberians land boundary centered between Colchis and Persia. The Iberians traded with the Greeks, the Carthaginians, and the Phoenicians. The Sicani tribe of Sicily were of Iberian origin. Carthage and Rome conscripted Iberians as mercenary troops. The cuisine of foods coming from this ancient region are such dishes as *bacalhau a bras* (codfish with eggs and potatoes), *bacalhau com nata* (cod cooked with cream), *longanitsa* stew, and *cocido montanes* (beans, cabbage, pork stew). Other mouth-watering dishes are *Cochinillo asado* and *lechazo* (roast piglet and roast lamb).

In 632 BCE, Cyrus the Great of Medo-Persia, together with Nabopolassar of Babylon, overthrew Assyria. By the time Xerxes I ruled on the throne of Persia in the fifth century BCE it was said the Persia Empire ruled from "India to Ethiopia", Persia having invaded the Kingdom of Kush in 530 BCE during the Twenty-fifth Dynasty when Kush ruled on Pharoah's throne. But just like every other army who entered the world stage as unstoppable, Persia would in time be humbled. The Greek Macedonians under Philip II emerged onto the world scene in the Balkan Peninsula. The Macedonians were descendants of Japheth. The ancient goldmine city of Phillipi was named after Phillip II. But when he was assassinated in 336 BCE his son Alexander succeeded him. Alexander the Great of Macedonia extended his father's kingdom and overthrew Persia, Egypt, and other kingdoms. Alexander built a mansion in Egypt, which he called Alexandria. But he never received the chance to reside there. Suddenly at the peak of his rule, Alexander the Great died at the age of thirty-two from malaria in 323 BCE. His empire was divided up among his four generals: General Cassander, who took over Macedonia and Greece; General Lysimachus, who controlled Asia Minor and Turkey; Seleucus Nicator, who was given Mesopotamia and Syria; and Ptolemy Lagus, who governed Egypt and Palestine. So one kingdom ended up becoming four kingdoms.

However, these four governments would themselves splinter and divide over time as the lineages of Japheth, Shem, and Ham continued to multiply. In 192 BCE war broke out in Greece. Syria came, not only to restore order, but also to grab more territory for itself. But another new political formation was watching, Rome, who declared war on Syria and defeated her. Following this, Rome later declared war on Macedonia in 167 BCE and overtook them. Not yet an empire, the Roman Republic's eventual climb to world domination would be gradual. Rome's system of government allowed for her citizens to be exempted from paying taxes. But not so true of the republic's provinces, who were taxed heavily. During his rule during the republic, Julius Caesar mentioned of a tribal-occupied territory beyond the Rhine, calling the tribes *Germania*. Another tribal area of concern to Rome were the Celtic tribes on the island *Britannia*, which later was invaded and became a Roman province. The peoples of both territories – *Germania and Britannia* – were also descendants of the brother Japheth, and so related to the other two brothers, Shem and Ham.

And just like all other nations prior, Rome created a slavery system. When Macedonia was conquered by Rome, thousands of Macedonians were sold into slavery. The province governors of Rome also supplied the slavery system by conducting man-hunts on the lower class in the provinces and thus, provide a steady supply of fresh raw slave labor. So instead of investing in their slaves and keeping them healthy as long as possible, Rome wore their slaves out physically until they were no longer useful and needed to be replaced with cheap new labor.

But the process of forcing a free people descending from one's forefathers into servitude always comes with a painful price – Rebellion. It was not any different with Rome. From 135 - 73 BCE, the Roman Republic experienced three slave rebellions, the last one causing panic that it might overtake Rome. They were called the Servile Wars. The first rebellion started with two slaves named Eunus and Cleon on the island of Sicily. Their army of slaves rose up and lasted three years, before Roman soldiers arrived in Sicily and defeated them. In 104 BCE another revolt for freedom broke out. It started with Consul Gaius Marius who was recruiting Roman soldiers for the war in the North. He requested support from Bithynia, a Roman province in Asia, but the king of Bithynia refused him, saying they were already slaves under Rome for being unable to pay their taxes to the republic. Gaius Marius reported the matter to the Senate, who declared that henceforth all allies of Rome to have their slaves immediately freed.

In obedience to the statute, about 800 enslaved humans were released and given freedom in Sicily. But the Sicilian plantation owners rejected the prospect of losing their free labor force. The statute in Sicily was quickly revoked, causing a rebellion among the 800 laborers who had been emancipated just days earlier. By the time 600 soldiers were sent to "restore order" the former slaves had spread out and began forming units of their own, under the leadership of a former slave named Salvius Tryphon. Under his leadership, other enslaved workers joined the units, which grew to 2,000 horsemen and 20,000 on foot. Another group under a slave named Athenion also joined Salvius' army. Two years went by, and the revolt was said to have grown to around 40,000 men. However, at the battle of Scirthaea, about half of Salvius Tryphon's army were struck down. Athenion was wounded and fell from his horse, but escaped. The final battle in Sicily came in 101 BCE and the Roman armies destroyed Athenion's army.

The third rebellion took place in 73 BCE. It started at a slave-gladiators school in Capua, Italy, where male slaves were trained to fight and participate in the Gladiator Games. But some 200 gladiators had planned to escape. However, on the day they had planned to take their flight to freedom they were betrayed and only 70 men were able to make flight, who seized wagons carrying weapons and armor. The 70 men later organized themselves and chose three leaders, Crixus, Oenomaus, and Spartacus. In two years they swayed other slaves to join them, their number swelling to 120,000 men, women, and children. The three leaders led their armies to several victories and raids. The Roman Republic became alarmed when the revolt reached

Campania, a vacation resort for the rich Romans. The Praetorian armies were sent to subdue them, but the gladiator slaves prevailed. In another battle, Oenomaus was alledgedly killed and Spartacus and Crixus divided into two armies. It was said there was fear Spartacus might march to the capital of Rome itself. In the spring of 72 BCE the Roman Legions were sent out near Mount Garganus against some 30,000 men. The thirty-thousand slaves were defeated and Crixus killed. The only leader left, Spartacus continued to outmaneuver the Roman legions, although losing men in subsequent battles. Making a deal with Cilician pirates, Spartacus looked to being transported to Sicily with 2,000 of his men and incite a slave revolt so to gather more recruits. But the pirates abandoned him and Spartacus retreated at Rhegium. Soon the legions under Marcus Licinius Crassus caught up with them. Spartacus tried to negotiate, but Crassus refused, causing some of Spartacus' men to break loose and flee towards the mountains. They were slaughtered. Spartacus and the rest of his men stood their ground and engaged one final time, before their struggle for freedom was put down and Spartacus killed. Slavery under Rome would be like iron, crushing.

Of the four kingdoms resulting from the breakup of Alexander's Greek empire, the kingdom under General Ptolemy Lagus lasted the longest. Governing the throne of Egypt, Ptolemy began his dynasty on Pharoah's throne. In 193 BCE, Antiochus III of Syria offered his daughter Cleopatra I in a political marriage alliance to Ptolemy V, designed to make Egypt subject to Syria through his daughter. However, Cleopatra subjected herself to her husband instead of to her father.

One hundred thirty years later, events occurring in Palestine unfolded. Rome marched into Jerusalem in 63 BCE. Jerusalem, where a carpenter named Jesus, who after being immersed by John the Baptist and became the "Great Teacher," was later executed by Pontius Pilate for preaching to the Jewish Nation and their religious leaders about a Messianic "Kingdom of God." According to the "*Book of the history of Jesus Christ, son of David, son of Abraham,*" written by Levi Matthew a former tax collector, Jesus was of the tribe of Judah and also a descendant of Shem, the brother of Ham and Japheth.

Jesus, who was also called "the Christ" was executed on Jewish Passover Day on the Hebrew month Nisan 14, 33 CE. Is there any historical evidence outside of the Bible that there was ever such a person named Jesus Christ? Was there a John the Baptist? Biblical writings speak of a Herod Antipas, a district ruler in Galilee whose scandalous wife Herodias arranged for the head of John the Baptist served on a platter. The ancient historian Josephus wrote in 93 CE: "To some of the Jews the destruction of Herod's army seemed to be divine vengeance, and certainly a just vengeance, for his treatment of John, *surnamed the Baptist.* For Herod had put him to death, though he was a good man and had exhorted the Jews to lead righteous lives."

Josephus also mentions of a Jesus, and who had a brother that was arrested: "convened the judges of the Sanhedrin and brought before them a man named James, the brother of Jesus *who was called the Christ*, and certain others." Roman historian Tacitus made this mention in his writings in 100 CE: "Christus, the founder of the name, had undergone the death penalty in the reign of Tiberius, *by sentence of the procurator Pontius Pilatus*, and the pernicious superstition was checked for a moment, only to break out once more, not merely in Judaea, the home of the disease, but in the capital itself." This is factual evidence of real historical persons who existed and experienced these events, attested by two known ancient historians.

Let us now turn our attention to the lineage of the third brother, Ham.

# CHAPTER THREE

# The Sons of Ham

**The sons of Ham were Mizraim, Put, Canaan, Cush, and Nimrod.**

LET US REVISIT AGAIN FOR a moment the legends of a global flood. The Sumerians of ancient Mesopotamia said that their gods decided to destroy mankind with a giant flood, but a man named Ziusudra was warned. He and his family were able to survive in a huge boat. The Moussaye tribe in Chad, Africa recite the story of a mother preparing a big meal for her family. At that time the sky was said to be so close in those days that one could reach up and touch the sky with their hand. As the mother was pounding the millet she lifted the pestle too high and poked a hole in the sky, causing a heavy rain that flooded the whole earth for seven days and seven nights. And the Arikara, an aboriginal Caddo Indian tribe of the Great Plains, United States (their language is nearly extinct, as Arikara is reported to be spoken by only 10 people), say that the earth was once inhabited by a race of strong giants who ridiculed the gods. The god Nesaru destroyed these giants by means of a flood but preserved his people, and the animals in a cave.

It is interesting how this legend permeates around the world. As the above examples show, the legend had even transferred from Africa to North America. Several researchers believe that ancient Africans explored the Americas, and there is strong presentable evidence that many say is certain proof. Other researchers are not yet convinced, and so this debate goes on (See Sources under Chapter Three, for more discussion). Here we will not explore and cover all the convincing evidence of an American exploration by Africans, and allow those who have the evidence in that field of study to do that. We will only add a few facts. Consider this: the earth is covered by seventy percent water. It has been said that if all the land above sea level were to be flattened out evenly, then water would cover the entire earth, one and one-half miles deep. Where did this water come from? Did a deluge of water once occur in mankind's ancient history which engulfed the earth? Now consider this thought: If there was a time on earth when oceans did not yet exist, then that would mean there was a time when people could cross from one land to another by simply walking there. There is a strong possibility that at one time there were no "volumes of water" that one had to cross. Were the continents also possibly closer to each other at one time? Did the continents begin to drift away? Of course there are critics to that view. Those who favor this theory could digress and remind their critics there were once people who believed the earth was flat.

Consider this as fact: The earth's continents *have* moved apart over geologic time. In 1596, a geologist by the name of Abraham Ortelius began to question if the continents were drifting. In his work "*Thesaurus Geographicus*" Ortelius speculated that the Americas were "torn away from Europe and Africa...by earthquakes and floods... The vestiges of the rupture reveal themselves if someone brings forward a map of the world and considers carefully the coasts of the three [continents]." In 1912, geologist Alfred Wegener invented the phrase "continental drift" based on his evidence. And the evidence today of plant and animal fossils found on different continents is available for anyone to inquire. Two examples being the fossils of the small crocodile called Mesosaurus, which is found not only in Brazil but also in South Africa, while several unique species of earthworms are in South America and Africa. We will explore the possibility of an African Expedition across the Atlantic later.

There is yet one more legend about a vessel carrying people to safety that we should examine. This account may be relevant to the evidence for the existence of an ancient man named Ham, known as the third son of Noah. The country where this legend originates may shock some – this story comes from a village in Abkhazia at a settlement called Adzyubzha.

The story is a folk legend: 'There was supposedly a slave ship that wrecked during a great storm along the Black Sea, and the slaves that survived were later sold in the area. The descendants of those sold survivors later founded a colony in Abkhazia.' However, there are two lingering questions about that folk story, which have never yet been answered – how did a ship ever enter the waters of the Black Sea, when the major shipping lanes of the slave trade were conducted far elsewhere? And also – when was this storm? What time period in history did it occur? Was this folk story alluding to the legend of the global flood? Another question even more thought-provoking: Does this thousand year oral narrative establish the possibility that there was a kingdom in the continent we call Africa, but whose borders encompassed an area that was in the region of Armenia? This entire discussion on the Abkhazians of African descent does lend weight to possible evidence of a "Land of Cush" near the Tigris and Euphrates Rivers in early human history, within the area of modern-day Armenia and Georgia. The possibility taps our imagination, and opens our minds to a totally different geographical map of the ancient world, in contrast to the taught history we know today.

The Abkhazians of African descent were announced to the 20th century world from a Russian magazine named *Argus,* in its March 6, 1913 issue, which said the existence of African descent people in Russia is a fact, and should "become scientific study" for all to know. A Russian scientist named P. Kovalevsky also wrote that what was most surprising and even strange for Russia was the fact there was a "whole village" inhabited by "Negroes." An Abkhazian linguist and ethnographer, Dmitri Gulia (1874 – 1960) according to his book "*The History of Abkhazia*" stated there are similar geographical names of villages, towns, and rivers between Abkhazia and Abyssino – Egyptian regions. The Russian writer Maxim Gorky visited Adzyubzha in 1927 and met some of the elderly Africans. Gorky came to the same opinion that the inhabitants in the African village were probably descendants of Africans from Ethiopia. It is true that Alexander the Great's Grecian empire did stretch from the Black Sea region to Ethiopia. So what about that local folk story of a slave ship that wrecked?

There are several theories to this folk story. One theory comes from Sergey Arutyunov, the head of the Division of Caucasian Nations at the Institute of Ethnology and Anthropology of the Russian Academy of Sciences. His conclusion was that during the late 18th or early 19th century CE, a slave ship traveling from Turkey to Crimea was caught in a storm and crashed off the coast of Abkhazia, whereupon Russian soldiers nearby saved the survivors, who were released from slavery and settled in Abkhazia. Arutyunov did admit that this event was a rare unique case. However, the question still begs to be answered – Why was a Turkish slave ship heading north to Crimea, when the main trade routes at that time had slaves being supplied from the Caucasus and Crimea *to the south,* and not vice versa? And what about this "great storm"? Why are there no details about it available? It should be noted at this point that the mountains of Ararat are nearby.

During the 1850's in a village called *T'Khina* in Abkhazia, an aboriginal woman who had auburn hair, muscular, six-foot, six inches tall, and could outrun a horse was reportedly "captured" in the mountainous forests. Her name was Zana, who was sold to a local nobleman, and worked for him as a house servant. Sadly, she was forced into the life of a sex slave, and gave birth to several children. Zana died in 1890, and four of her children reached adulthood, married, and had their own families. Between 2010 – 2013, a research project to determine Zana's aboriginal roots by DNA testing was conducted, which included Zana's descendants. The testing was headed by Bryan Sykes, a professor of human genetics at the University of Oxford. According to Professor Sykes, the test results showed the woman Zana, who was found in the forests of a village in Abkhazia, was "100% SubSaharan African."

In a separate research project, the European Journal of Human Genetics, volume 24, published a study in 2015 entitled *"Genetic evidence for an origin of the Armenians from Bronze Age mixing of multiple populations."* While testing for Armenian genetic mixture relationship to worldwide populations, the study showed that the oldest mixture events appeared to be between populations related to sub-Saharan Africans and West Europeans, and which occurred around 3800 BCE. This was well before the Slave Trade began.

In connection with this comes another story from the folklore of Abkhazia, the several thousand year old legend of *The Narts*, a European people of the Caucasus region. As this legend unfolds: 'the tribe traveled night and day for *18 months*. They pitched camp under a tree and made a fire to cook, like they always had. But this time, the smoke from their camp traveled a half day's distance and came to the attention of a black-skinned people, who followed the smoke and came upon the people from the Caucasus. The black-skinned people made the Narts their guests and spread a big feast. After one month, the Narts began to prepare their return back to the Caucasus region. One hundred of the best black-skinned horsemen desired to go back with them to see how they lived.'

This legend corroborates that a migration had taken place of Ham's descendants into the continent we today call Africa.

Ham's son Nimrod founded the kingdoms of Erech, Akkad, Calneh, and Babel. Ham's son Mizraim and his descendants in time migrated to an eastern portion of a continental landmass along the Nile River. Eventually a kingdom called *Kemet* was born. It had two sovereign states – Mehew (Northland) and Ta-Meh (Land of Reeds). The inhabitants called themselves *Kemetiu*.

According to the writings of Manetho, a Hamitic priest who lived in the Third Century BCE, a Mizraim-descended leader named Menes united the two lands into one kingdom, became the first pharaoh, and founded the city "Menfe" in Mehew, the lower region of the Kemet Kingdom. The city Menfe is said to have been founded in the Third Millennium. Let us now momentarily pause and ask this question: What became the modern-day name for Kemet, and how did that come about?

The capital of Kemet was Menfe. This capital was also known by other names, such as *Inebu-hedj*, meaning "White Walls", and *Ankh-Tawy* which meant "Life of the Two Lands." But there was another name the city was known by – *Hwt-Ka-Ptah*, meaning "Home of the Spirit of Ptah." This was because the city Menfe was home to the temple of the so-called god Ptah. The Greeks referred to Menfe by calling the city by the temple's name, Hwt-Ka-Ptah. However, they pronounced it as *A-ku-pi-ti-yo* and spelled it *Aigyptos*. Today the word has made its way into our anglicized version "Egypt." This was how the Land of Kemet became known today as Egypt. Some of the culinary tastes of Egypt today include *Shawarma* (grilled lamb or chicken rolled in flatbread with tomato and onions), Kebab sausage kofta, and *Mulukhiyah* soup with rabbit or lamb.

Kemet was a powerful kingdom for many centuries, and the home of their supreme monarch, the Pharoah. The priest-historian Manetho compiled the chronological reigns of the Pharoahs in his written work entitled *"Aegyptiaca"* (History of Egypt). He divided this work into three volumes, listing Kemet's dynasty of rulers, starting with Pharoah Menes, who was legendary in unifying the twenty Nomes (districts/cities) in Lower Egypt and the twenty-two Nomes in Upper Egypt, which bordered Nubia / Kush / Sudan. Kemet was highly advanced in several areas, including astronomy and mathematics, one example being the measurements they took from the stars to align their pyramids with the cardinal points of the earth. Kemet also developed a 365-day calendar, used to determine the annual flooding of the Nile, and the number of hours between the sunset and sunrise.

In the Nubia region south of Kemet on its border was the Kingdom of Kerma, in present-day Sudan. The Kerma Kingdom was an early civilization in Nubia, and lasted for about one thousand years, from 2500 to 1500 BCE. Another culture that migrated into the Nile Delta area of Nubia were the Hyksos, a people of Semitic-speaking origin. Around 1650 BCE the Hyksos invaded Kemet, and with that victory became the Fifteenth Dynasty of Kemet for about one hundred years. However, in Kerma was yet another developing culture that would soon emerge, the Kingdom of Kush, which will later be discussed.

One of Mizraim's sons was Lehabim. In time, his descendants roamed as tribes in the regions west of Kemet. These many tribes west of Kemet spoke Amazigh, a branch of the AfroAsiatic language family. These descendant groups, stretching from Mali and the

Niger River, to the southern border of the Mediterranean Sea, and spread through the Sub-Sahara, were also called Amazighs. One of the Amazigh populous were the Libu. Ancient Kemet called them "Tjehenu." The Libu were shepherding nomads, and were attested to in the writings dating to the Pharaohs of the Nineteenth Dynasty of Egypt during the 13th Century BCE.

The Greeks called the Amazighs "Berbers", while the Romans called them "Libyans." The term "Berber" was a variation of the Greek word "Barbaros (Barbarian). In time, some of the Berbers would later be referred in Latin as the *Mauri*.

The Libu Princes and Shoshenq I founded the Libyan Dynasty, a part of that Libu reign becoming the Twenty-Second Dynasty of Egypt (945 – 745 BCE). The Libyan Dynasty were contemporaries with the Nubian Kingdom of Kush, and the Kingdom of Carthage. How did the famed city of Carthage come about?

Ham's son Canaan had a firstborn son named Sidon. Sidon's descendants eventually became known as Sidonians. Sometime prior to the 15th Century BCE the Sidonians established a colony in Amazigh-Berber territory and named the seaport town Sidon. Another Sidonian colony would soon be formed about 22 miles away. The name of that seaport would be called Tyre. Both seaports Tyre and Sidon became trading centers where traveling caravans and merchant ships came to engage in trading. The Sidonians in Amazigh-Berber territory also became well known for their skills as shipbuilders, metalworkers, artisans, and craftsmen in glassware, weaving, and engraving. The Greeks who sailed into their seaports began calling the Sidonians by the name "Phoenicians." The Phoenicians (the Sidonians) and Berbers began doing business together. In time, other settlements were founded by the Phoenicians in Berber territory, including Carthage, which was located on the coast of present-day Tunisia. At first, the Berber chieftains commanded respect from the newly arrived Phoenician immigrants, as Carthage paid tax to the Berber kingdoms.

But as time went on, the Phoenicians' material resources kept increasing, and the developing city of Carthage began to influence the Berber region politically and economically. The Greek village of *Oea* later changed hands to the Phoenicians, who founded the city of *Oyat* (Tripoli) in the 7th century BCE. The Berber settlement of Tunis was also incorporated into Carthage, who expanded by the 5th century BCE in acquiring productive Berber farmlands. Wealthy trading clients also began migrating into Phoenician territory to do business. This change in economic status between the Berbers and the Phoenicians resulted in bad blood. Despite intermarriage between the two cultures, the Berbers engaged in revolts against Carthage during the 4th century.

The names of some of the Amazigh – Berber kingdoms were Garamantia, Numidia, and Mauretiania, whom the Romans called the "Mauri" (the Moors). Numidia ( 4th Century - 202 BCE) was located in present-day Algeria and part of Tunisia and Libya. Today a specialty dish in these regions is *Pastilla* pie, slow-cooked spiced poultry pastilla and spicy seafood pastilla. Another favorite North African dish is the cooking-pot stew called *Tajine*, made of meat, chicken, or fish, with vegetables or fruit, nuts, and spices of ginger, cumin, turmeric, and other flavors. A taste of Moroccan coffee with cinnamon, nutmeg, clove, and cardamon seeds is a brewed drink for any time of the day. The Berber kingdoms traded with Carthage, shared borders alongside Carthage, and served as mercenary soldiers for them. This Berber kingdom became a Roman province in 202 BCE. Eventually, however, the main conflict among regional rivals turned out to be war with Rome in the Punic Wars. The First War began in 264 BCE when a local conflict in Sicily turned into a full-scale war between Carthage and Rome over Sicily, no thanks to the Italian mercenary pirates called the Mamertines. Carthage and Rome made peace in 241, despite Carthage's refusal to release Roman prisoners. The Second War began a little over twenty years later, after Carthage's conquest of Iberia. This was caused in 219 BCE when neighboring tribal allies of Carthage were attacked and massacred by fighters from the town of Saguntum. Hannibal retaliated and attacked Sanuntum, a protectorate of Rome. When Carthage refused to hand Hannibal over, Rome declared war. This conflict resulted in Rome battling Carthage in three locations – Iberia, Sicily, and Italy, when Hannibal crossed the Alps with three dozen elephants and soldiers, invading Italy and defeating the Romans there in 218 BCE. However, the war spilled over into Carthage's home region in 202 BCE, where their territory was eventually reduced to only the city of Carthage remaining. A Peace Treaty was agreed upon.

The Peace Treaty included that Carthage pay annually 200 silver talents for fifty years to Rome, as well as seeking approval from the Roman Senate before taking military action of any sort. Carthage fully fulfilled the former in 151 BCE, but ignored the latter, caused by a war clash with Numidia. In 149 BCE, looking for an opportunity to conquer Carthage and control the rich resources of the land, Rome put demands on Carthage, such as promising to render over all weapons, as well as offering three hundred Carthaginian children. Carthage agreed to meet the demands, in return for their land rights and sovereignty recognized. But the last demand – move at least 16 kilometers to the interior and allow the city to be burned down – caused Carthage to withdraw from further talks. Rome declared War again.

A three year Roman siege on the city of Carthage resulted. After strong resistance waned by the year 146, the Roman military finally made Carthage an occupation with 50,000 Carthaginians sold into slavery and the city set on fire for 17 days. The site of Tunisia today became sadly then annexation, and a source of food supply to Rome. Carthage was rebuilt, made a province of Rome, and the region was renamed *Africa* at a time **before the continent was even called Africa.** This is proven because the available world maps at that time show the continent was called *Libya*, not Africa (See pictures).

So where did the word *Africa* originate? There have been various theories put forth, the strongest asserting that the word came either from the Egyptian language word *Afruika*, meaning Spirit, or the Berber-Libyan language word *Afri*, meaning "Cave/Tunnel," a fitting descriptive word of the mountainous terrain in certain geographic regions of North Africa.

The Kingdom of Kush was an ancient kingdom in Nubia (Sudan). Its first capital was Napata, followed by Meroe. In Meroe the right of kingship was matriarchal through the female family line rather than the male line. Nubia was made a colony of Kemet, when it was annexed by Kemet in the 16th Century BCE Nubia and Kemet became culturally identical, the early history of Nubia dating back to Mentuhotep II of the 21st Century BCE. In the writings of Amenhotep I and Ahmose, the Kushites in time resisted Kemet rule and were described as "Bowmen." After two hundred years of rule with the Twenty-second Dynasty of Egypt by the Libyan Princes, the Kushite king Kashta took over Upper Egypt at Thebes. Kashta's successor, Piye, later took control of Lower Egypt at Memphis. Thus, the 25th Dynasty of Egypt began in the 8th Century, with the Kings of Kush sitting on Pharoah's throne. King Piye's inscriptions found at the Egyptian temple of Amun drew attention to his victory celebration. The Victory Stele of King Piye at Amun's temple states: "Amun of Napata granted me to be ruler of every foreign country...Amun of Thebes granted me to be ruler of the Black Land."

King Piye's son was Taharqa. The 25$^{th}$ Dynasty reached its peak under Taharqa, who is credited with reviving the glory and prosperity of ancient Egypt. Circa 732 BCE, Taharqa deployed his armies to call out the Assyrians to battle. That historical fact is cited in the Book of Kings in the Greek *Septuagint*. According to the account, this occurred during the same moment that Assyria was attempting to besiege the two-tribe Kingdom of Judah during the reign of Hezekiah. Assyria had already captured Samaria, capital of the ten-tribes of Israel, and other northern Jewish cities. But the Assyrians were not finished. They relished the capture of Jerusalem in Palestine, and surrounded the city with troops. Ancient historians, however, did not view the boasts of the Sennacherib Prism as convincing proof that Jerusalem was really captured by Assyria. General Sennacherib, the son of Assyrian King Sargon II, boasted: "As to Hezekiah, the Jew, he did not submit to my yoke…Himself I made a prisoner in Jerusalem, his royal residence, like a bird in a cage." Sennacherib's Prism went on to state that Hezekiah had paid him a tribute of 800 talents of silver, inferring that Jerusalem had surrendered.

But historian Herodotus of the 5$^{th}$ Century BCE claimed the city had not been captured by Assyrian soldiers, but instead had to abandon their invasion because: "one night a multitude of fieldmice swarmed over the Assyrian camp and devoured their quivers and their bows and the handles of their shields." Another claim in regards to Sennacherib's siege of Jerusalem comes from historian Josephus of the 1$^{st}$ Century. Quoting the Babylonian Berossus, Josephus stated: "When Senacheirimos returned to Jerusalem from his war with Egypt, he found there the force under Rapsakes in danger from a plague, for God had visited a pestilential sickness upon his army, and on the first night of the siege one hundred and eighty-five thousand men perished with their commanders and officers." Notably, the

Book of Kings also mentions the number of 185,000 dead Assyrian troops on that night, not however by disease, but by "One Angel" of God. Combining all these historical sources does seem to testify that something "Unusually Strange" happened the night that Jerusalem was surrounded by Assyrian soldiers.

Sennacherib's successor was Esarhaddon, who invaded Egypt during Kush's reign, but Kush's leader Taharqa was able to escape. Taharqa's successor Tantamani and his Kushite warriors retook Memphis. But Ashurbanipal of Assyria and his forces provoked another war in 663 BCE, preventing Tantamani from remaining on Pharoah's throne, forcing him to return to Nubia. Queens also ruled Kush in its history. The title "Candace" was used by several queens. One of such queens was Amanirenas, whose battles with the Romans in Egypt for five years (27 BCE – 22 BCE) led to a Kush victory. Kush traded iron products with the Romans, along with gold, ivory, and slaves.

Eventually, Kush began to fade as an international power. Around 350 CE the Kingdom of Aksum conquered Kush. The Kingdom of Aksum, also known as Axum or the Aksumite Empire, was centered in the region of present-day Eritrea, Ethiopia, Yemen, Sudan, Egypt, and Saudi Arabia.

The Kingdom of Aksum is attested by the *Periplus of the Erythraean Sea*, a document written in the 1st Century CE:

"Opposite Mountain Island, on the mainland twenty stadia from shore, lies Adulis, a fair-sized village, from which there is a three-days' journey to Coloe, an inland town and the first market for ivory. From that place to the city of the people called **Auxumites** there is a five days' journey more; to that place all the ivory is brought from the country beyond the Nile through the district called Cyeneum, and thence to Adulis."

Besides the "Auxumites" being mentioned was also another ancient African city called Adulis, which today would be located in the
modern city of Zula, Eritrea.

Aksum became a major player on the commercial trade route
between Egypt and India. The Aksumite rulers facilitated trade by
minting their own currency. Aksum exported frankincense and
myrrh. Ships passing between Egypt and India would also stop
at the Himyarite Kingdom in Yemen, involved in the spice trade.
Himyarite, established in 110 BCE, was once part of the Sabaen
people of Saudi Arabia, whose ancestor was Seba, one of the sons
of Cush, son of Ham. Subsequently, Aksum saw an opportunity to
extend their rule over its east African region, by making a move to
conquer Himyarite. So in 525 CE., the Aksumite general Abraha deposed the viceroy of Himyarite and withheld tribute to King Kaleb,
with the support of Ethiopians who had settled in Yemen. Abraha
held off two attempts to remove him, resulting in Yemen being under
Aksum's rule. After Abraha's death years later, his son Masruq Abraha
became the next viceroy in Yemen. However, his half-brother Ma'd-
Karib revolted and called upon the Emperor of Persia, Khosrow I, to
step in and give his support. The armies of Persia, in the form of 800
men, came up against Aksum in 570 CE, killing Masruq Abraha, and
expelling Aksum from the Arabian Peninsula. However, from 575 –
578 CE. began the Persian Wars between Persia and Aksum, which
was sparked when Persia's vassal king was killed by the Ethiopians in
Yemen. This time, Persia came with 4,000 men, and Aksum retreated
from Yemen's internal affairs.

After the Persian Wars, Aksum, though weakened, remained a
strong empire and trading power until the rise of Islam in the 7th
Century. Aksum later went into economic isolation, eventually ceas-

ing its production of coins in the early 7th Century. An example of Aksum's influential presence in the international trade of its day can be seen from Aksum's King Ezana, whose minted gold coins under his reign have been unearthed at archeologial sites in India during the late 1990's. The coins he circulated carried the motto "May this please the people." Aksum King Ouazebas also contained this same motto on his gold coins that were in circulation in his day.

In quick review, we have stretched across the breath of North Africa and have examined the ancient people and history of Libya, Carthage, Kush, Aksum, and Kemet. Other descendants of Ham throughout the continent later called *Africa* were also building civilizations and developing trade routes both domestically and internationally, such as Kongo, Nigeria, Ghana, Mali, and South Africa.

What other continent did the descendants of Ham migrate to in ancient times?

Egyptian Pyramid. Great Sphinx of Giza and the Pyramid tomb of Khafre, on the outskirts of Cairo. The pyramids were built not only for burial tombs, but also as yearly calendars.

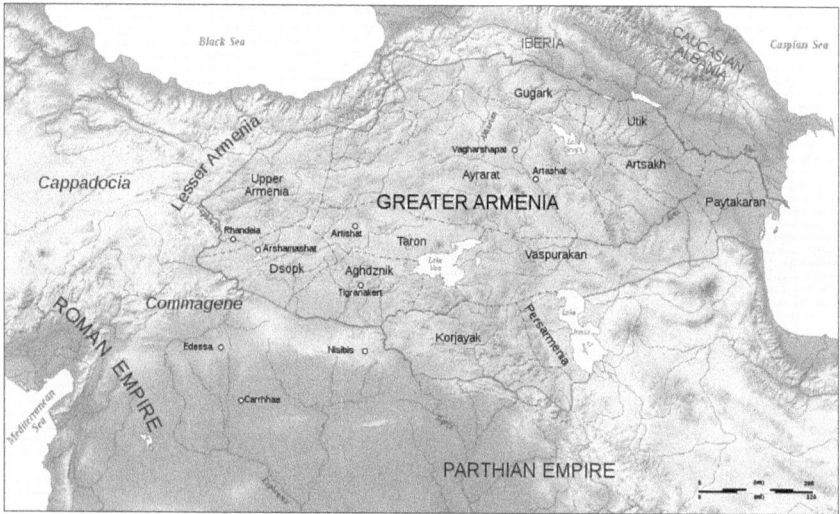

Armenia Map. According to the ancient biblical account, the Ark, built by three brothers and their father Noah, rested on the mountain ranges in Armenia. Hundreds of cultures around the world have legends of a global deluge and only a few survivors. The Euphrates and Tigris Rivers both have its source in Armenia.

Abkyasian Family. For over 100 years, researchers have tried to discover the origin of the dark-skinned Abkyasians, in the city of Abkhazia, Georgia Republic, on the east coast of the Black Sea. The legend of the garden of Eden reported a Land of Cush encircled near the Euphrates River.

Tunis. A city in Tunisia, North Africa. Picture taken in 1899. The area in ancient times was once part of a mighty kingdom called Carthage.

Venice, Italy. A gondola on the Grand Canal.

Greek man. Greece played a major part in world history.

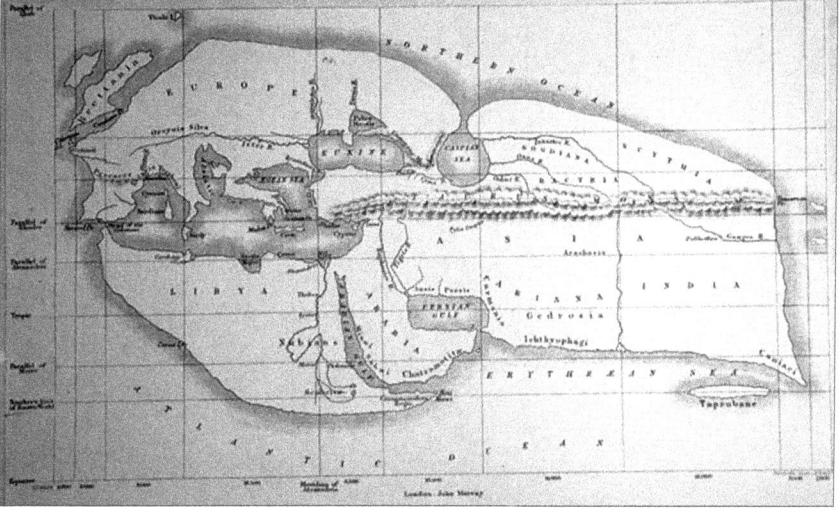

Map of the World in 194 BCE, by the Greek geographer Eratosthenes. Notice a continent called *Libya*, before it was later called Africa.

Tripoli today, a city in Libya.

Chinese Family in Hong Kong, 1869.

Manchu Ladies at a meal table, 1869.

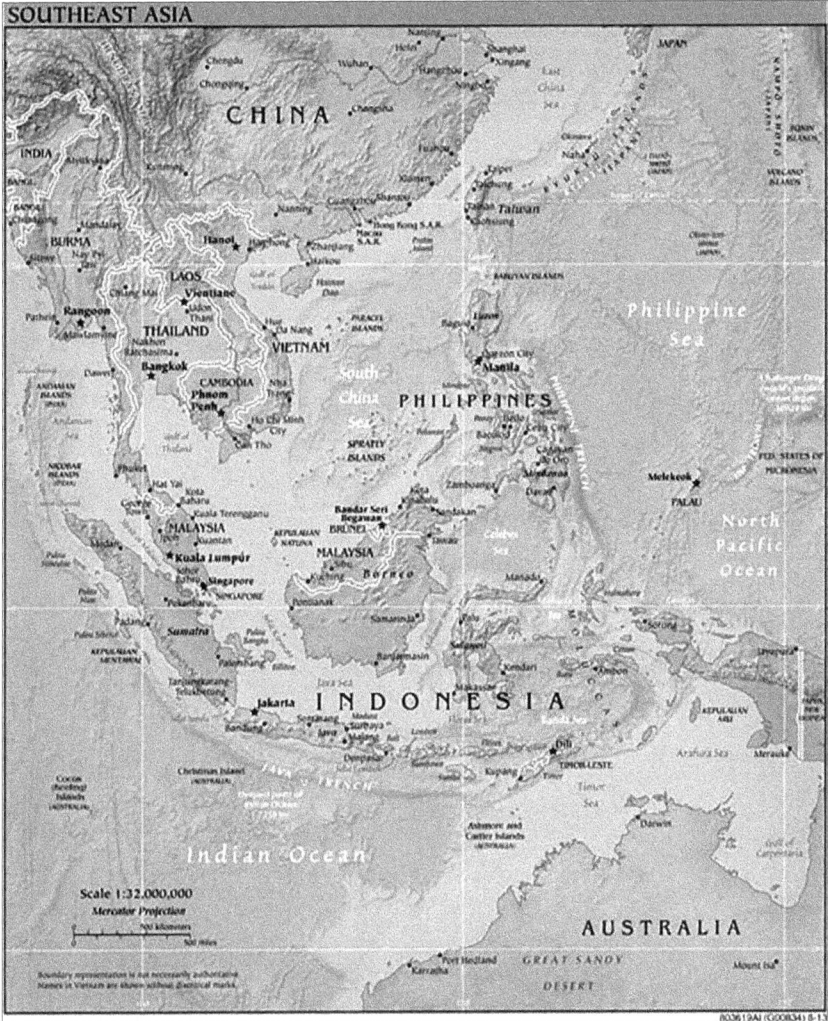

Map of SE Asia

Indigenous People Today

Olmec Head in Mexico. Found in San Lorenzo, Veracruz State, Mexico. Displayed in the Xalapa Museum of Anthropology.

Olmec Head. The first colossal head was discovered in 1862 in Veracruz, Mexico by Jose Maria Melgar y Serano.

CAPT CROKER HORROR STRICKEN AT ALGIERS, on witnessing the Miseries of the Christian Slaves chaind & in Irons driven home after labour by Infidels with large Whips.    Page ibid

1815 illustration of white slaves in Algiers, Algeria. The enslavement of Europeans was once part of the East African Slave Trade. North African Barbary chiefs plowed the seas to pirate unsuspecting ships and raid coastal towns for their supply of slaves.

# CHAPTER FOUR

# When Did Africa and China Make First Contact?

W<small>HAT OTHER CONTINENT DID THE</small> descendants of Ham migrate to besides the continent of *Libya* which later was called *Africa* by the Romans?

In this chapter, convincing evidence will be presented in relation to that question. However, in order to answer that intriguing question, we must first find the answer to this thought-provoking one – When did Africa and China first make contact with each other? Let us examine this.

East African merchant Zhengjiani and his trade party traveled to China in 1071 and was received by Chinese Emperor Shenzong. The emperor gave Zhengjiani the title "Lord Guardian of Prosperity", revealing the deep bonds of trade and commerce between the two of them. Zhengjiani and his merchant delegates returned again to China in 1081.

The Chinese admiral and navigator Zheng He explored the coast of East Africa in the year 1416 during the Ming Dynasty, and visited Mogadishu, present-day Somalia. Zheng He's sailing charts of forty pages, called the *Mao Kun* Map, cover four areas – Sri Lanka, South India, Maldives, and 400 kilometers of the east coast of Africa. The ancient Chinese also developed, during the Ming Dynasty, a map of the African continent in 1389, which is noted for including the southern tip of the continent around present-day South Africa. These facts show that cartography of Africa existed in ancient China.

In the year 813, according to the Chinese archives of the Tang Dynasty, in the *New Dynastic History of T'ang*, Book CCXXII, under the section *The Ho-ling Kuo Tiao* is found the following entry:

*"In the eighth year of the Yuan Ho period, the land of Ho-ling presented four Seng-chih slaves."*

This Chinese document contains an important clue. On the East coast of Africa is the country Zanzibar, settled by Bantu-speakers during the first millennium and originally called *Zanj* which means *Country of the Blacks*. Zanj for centuries shipped slaves to many kingdoms bordering the Indian Ocean. Those enslaved and traded to these countries were also referred to as *Zanj* slaves, designating their origin. The supply of slaves coming out of East Africa was part of the East African Slave Trade that flourished for centuries, even longer than the Atlantic Slave Trade (See Chapter Five). That official entry in the archives of the Tang Dynasty during the year 813 reveals that the four enslaved servants China received were from Zanj. The land of *Ho-ling* who presented China with four servants was the present-day country of Java in Indonesia. The regional trading routes of Zanj, or Zanzibar, stretched not only to China, but even to the Indonesian islands and Iran (Persia). This also demonstrates that both China and Africa shared mutual interests in the Indian Ocean trade.

Another word used in China to describe a person who was black and dark-skinned or a dark-skinned slave was the Chinese word *Kunlun*, found in their fiction and nonfiction literature.

In the *Chu Fan Chih* (Information about Barbarians) during

the year 1226, the following entry show the words Kunlun and Zanj combined together:

"The Land of *K'un-lun Ts'eng-ch'i* is situated on the shores of the Southwestern Sea behind a screen of large islands…the products of the land consist of elephant tusks and rhinoceros' horns. To the west there is an island peopled with savages whose complexion is like black lacquer and whose tresses resemble wriggling tadpoles. They are captured by using food as a bait, and are sold at great profit to the Arabs as slaves. The Arabs entrust them with their keys, knowing that they will be faithful be-cause they have no kith nor kin."

During the time of the Liu Song Dynasty in the fifth century, the term Kunlun was mentioned in an account about a kunlun slave named Bai Zhu, who stood at the emperor's side and who took orders from the emperor to beat ministers and officials with a stick. The name Bai was a common surname for non-Chinese people. Another example is found in a famous romance novel in China, written by Pei Xing in 880, called "The Kunlum Slave", when the black slave Mo-le, and his superhuman strength, rushes to save Cui's lover from the harem of a court official. The slave Mo-le leaped over ten walls with both of them on his back to safety. When the official learns of the escape he orders Mo-le to be captured, but Mo-le jumps over the city walls and is never seen again until ten years later selling medicine in the city.

However, were the presence of East Africans living in China only due to slavery? Did the word "Kunlun" apply only to African slaves? From the Chinese archives, the *Lin-yi Kuo Chuan*, ("Topography of the Land of Linyi") contained in Book 197 of the *Chiu T'ang Shu* ("Old Dynastic History of T'ang") in the year 945 said this:

"The people living to the south of Linyi have woolly hair and black skin, and are commonly known as K'unlun."

In the section titled *Chen-la Kuo Chuan* (Topography of the Land of Chen-la) found in the same book *Chiu Tang Shu*, we find the following:

"Chen-la is situated to the north-west of Lin-yi. It was formerly a dependency of Fu Nan. Its inhabitants belong to the race of K'un-lun."

The land of Linyi was Vietnam, and Chen-la represented the Khmer Empire, which later became Cambodia and parts of Vietnam, Laos, and Thailand. In volume X of the same work, we read: "The northern frontier of the land of K'un-lun…The country abounds in ebony, sandalwood, spices, glazed wares, crystal, medicinal herbs, precious stones."

In the *Wang Wu Tien Chu Kuo Chuan* (A Record of travels in the Five Indies) by Hui Ch'ao, we read one more reference about Kun-lun. : "To reach India and K'unlun, one must go by way of Gandahara." In another section it says : "Voyages from the Western Sea to the Southern Seas are frequently made for the purpose of procuring precious merchandise from Ceylon and gold from K'unlun, and they even sail as far as Canton to secure silk and other textiles."

Another reference is found in the year 684 in the ancient work *Jiu Tang shu* (Former Tang history), containing the phrase the "Kunlun of Guangzhou" (Canton). All of the above-cited texts clearly show that the word Kunlun referred not only to enslaved Africans, but also referred to Chinese communities in China and also to other Asian peoples. Two questions now arise: Why was the word Kunlun – which was synonymous with dark-skinned Africans – also being applied to populations in China, Southeast Asia and Indonesia? Was there evidence that ancient Chinese people had applied that word to themselves?

During the time of the Jin Dynasty, Emperor Fei was deposed in 371, and so Prime Minister Sima Yu replaced him, becoming the 8th emperor and receiving the official name "Emperor Jianwen" in 372. His reign did not last long. By the summer of that same year Emperor Jianwen became ill and soon died, only a few months after he took the throne. His younger concubine wife Li Lingrong out-lived him, who later became Empress dowager in 394 at the age of forty-three. But what is of more interesting note about Empress dowager Li is what the Jin archives recorded about her. According to the History of the Jin, it described Empress Li this way: **"She was tall and her coloring was black. All the people in the palace used to call her Kunlun."** Here we find direct evidence that the word "Kunlun" was applied to a Chinese person, even a Chinese Imperial Empress. How did Empress Li originally become a part of the Emperor Jianwen's royal house? Li Lingrong, born in 351, had become a servant girl in his household as a weaver. After the Emperor's concubines were no longer able to conceive anymore, Li Lingrong was selected to become his next concubine and conceive his heir, at the age of ten. She produced two sons and a daughter during their relationship.

So as early as the 4th Century the word Kunlun applied to dark-skinned Chinese. Empress Li at her death was officially mourned with ceremony pomp and honorably remembered by her people, so the word Kunlun carried no negative connotation during that time, since the Chinese Archives made no attempt to hide her physical description of being dark-skinned.

Were early rulers of ancient China the descendants of Ham? Some researchers have said that the Shang and Xia Dynasties had Black rulers who were called *Xuan Di* which when translated means

"Black Emperor." The symbol of the Shang clan was the bird. According to the Shang poem titled *Xuan Ciao*: "Heaven bade the *dark bird* to come down and bear the Shang." There are other examples pointing to evidence of an African presence in early Chinese history, one more example being the dark-skin Yi tribe of China, particularly in Guizhou, Yunnan, and Sichuan territory, who practiced a caste slavery system.

The Yi tribe divided themselves into Black Yi and White Yi. The Black Yi were the highest rank of society. They were the slave-owning class, who owned 60 to 70 percent of the arable land. They claimed their blood to be "pure" and forbade intermarriage with the White Yi or to the Ajia (slaves). Also too – a Black Yi without slaves or a poor Black Yi – was still higher in society than any White Yi, even to a wealthy White Yi. The Black Yi ruled by force. On the other hand, the White Yi were under the slave system, yet they could enjoy some economic independence. They had no freedom of migration, so they could not leave their assigned areas without permission from the Black Yi. They also had no right of ownership, but subject to restrictions by their masters. Although a Black Yi would not kill a White Yi, the Black Yi could still transfer his ownership control over a White Yi. Finally, there were the Ajia, the slaves, who could be sold, purchased, and killed without reprisal. Both the White Yi and Ajia slaves did all the farming and cultivation, while the Black Yi did only the administrative and military work. The Yi tribal slave system finally ended in 1949 during the Chinese Revolution. What is the accepted belief and history of the origin of the Chinese?

Chinese mythology held that the Chinese people were descendants of the Yellow Emperor. The most recent research holds that several different races of humans evolved separately and apart from each other at the same time throughout the continents. Chinese school curriculum teach that they evolved from the "Peking Man." However, in January 2005, a breakthrough study was reported by the China News Service – *DNA testing proved that the first populations of China were from Africa, particularly from the coast of East Africa.* The testing study was conducted by Chinese DNA specialist Jin Li, professor of both the National Human Genome Center in Shanghai and the Institute of genetics of Fudan University. Professor Li said the initial purpose and goal of the study was to try and confirm that the Chinese had evolved from the Chinese homo erectus independently of all humans, and the 12,000 DNA samples from 165 different ethnic groups would prove it Instead, the testing revealed something else – that not even one single person of Chinese descent who participated in the test could be considered as a descendant of homo erectus, because their DNA matched *African ethnic groups.* The Y-chromosome haplotypes of males from all parts of East Asia, including northern & southern Han, Tibetan, Hui, Mongolian, Korean, Japanese, Yao, Zhuang, Dong Taiwanese, and Southeast Asia: Vietnamese, Laotian, Kampuchean, Thai, Malay, and Javanese. All are derived from ancestral haplotypes that only exist in African populations.

The conclusion: China's ancestors were African. And those ancestors would be from the family line of Ham, the brother of Japtheth and Shem. For the first time there is now "scientific evidence" that matches the Chinese archival texts of "Black Emperors" in early Chinese history, and, a definitive explanation for the origin of the mysterious word *Kunlun*. Is there a legend in China about a worldwide storm that flooded mankind except for a few survivors? Interestingly, the Chinese word for *ship* in Chinese characters literally means *Eight mouths on a vessel*. This matches the original account Moses wrote, that eight persons survived a global deluge on a large vessel.

The route of Ham's family began in European Armenia, his

descendants to Africa, and from there to Southeast Asia, the Indus Valley, and next to China. Other African haplogroups, such as the *Negrito* would continue to migrate – to the Andaman Islands, the Philippines, Papua New Guinea, the aboriginals of Australia, and also to the Pacific Islands. When commenting on the DNA study, Professor Li stated the test results showed that all humans from different parts of the world are "very close relatives."

So we go back to the original question – when did Africa and China make first contact? We now understand the answer – the Chinese *came* from Africans, based on genetic science – DNA. Africans founded ancient China.

Yet, what other continent might the Africans have settled in, or discovered during their thirst for exploration? Could African vessels have reached *The Americas* in ancient times? Portuguese mariners during the late 15th century discovered a navigational technique called *Volta do mar* (meaning - turn of the sea/return from the sea), which required the ship's pilot to sail far to the west to catch the trade winds, and use them again by sailing north on the return trip. Did Africans have knowledge of these winds? During the 14th century in 1310, Abubakari II the king of the Mali Empire decided to commandeer an expedition himself and fulfill a dream since his boyhood – travel from Africa to explore the end of the Ocean. Special boats were built to survive a long voyage as this, and provisions were stocked that would last at least two years. Abubakari instructed his boat captains of the fleet to keep in constant contact during the expedition by means of the talking drums, and issued an order: "Do not return until you have reached the end of the ocean, or when you have exhausted your food and water." Before the king and his fleet departed in 1311, Abubakari conferred regency to his brother Kankan Musa with the understanding that Kankan assume the throne if he did not return. Kankan's brother King Abubakari never returned. Kankan Musa ascended the throne in 1312. Did Abubakari, or any other ancient African expedition, succeed in reaching the American continents?

The Norse explorer Leif Erikson supposedly was the first known European to have discovered North America at the northern tip of present-day Newfoundland, Canada in 999. According to the two sagas written about his travels, Erikson was originally heading to Greenland from Norway, when he was caught in strong winds and was blown off course. After several days at sea, Erikson accidently came upon a land which he named *Vinland*. In 1492, Columbus left Spain to try and find a westward route to Asia. After him, an Italian navigator named Amerigo Vespucci left Spain with a fleet of three ships to explore the landmass that Columbus had reached earlier. Vespucci reached Guyana, South America in 1499, and later realized this was not Asia, as Columbus claimed, but was a new continent.

One not well-known fact about Columbus' first voyage was that the person he chose to pilot the ship *Santa Maria* was Pedro Alonso Nino, who was a Moor. He was born in Palos de Moguer, Spain. Pedro and his three brothers were known as the Nino Brothers, all experienced sailing navigators. Pedro Alonso Nino gained part of his experience from exploring the coasts of Africa. His brother Juan Nino was the master of *La Nina*, another of the three Spanish ships on the first Columbus voyage. It was said that all three ships, the *Santa Maria*, the *Pinta*, and *La Nina*, were not built for the ocean, but mainly for sailing the Mediterranean Sea.

According to the abstract of Columbus's journal made by Bartolome de Las Casas, the objective of the third voyage was to verify the existence of a continent that King John II of Portugal suggested was located to the southwest of the Cape Verde Islands. King John reportedly knew of the existence of such a mainland because *"canoes had been found which set out from the coast of Guinea [West Africa] and sailed to the west with merchandise."* The Columbus abstract, made by Bartolome de Las Casas, continued to say:

> *"he [Columbus] would navigate, the Lord pleasing, to the west, and from there would go to this Española, in which route he would prove the theory of the King John aforesaid; and that he thought to investigate the report of the Indians of this Española who said that there had come to Española from the south and south-east, a black people who have the tops of their spears made of a metal which they call guanine, of which he had sent samples to the Sovereigns to have them assayed, when it was found that of 32 parts, 18 were of gold, 6 of silver and 8 of copper."*

*Guanín* is an alloy of copper, gold and silver, similar to red gold, used in pre-Columbian central America. *Guanín* has been in use in the Caribbean basin since at least the 1st century, if not earlier. Curious about the validity of this story, Columbus did indeed send samples of these spears back on a mail ship to Spain to be examined, and it was found that the ratio of properties of gold, copper, and silver alloy were identical to the spears that were being forged in African Guinea.

Did Africans know about the trade winds and the Canary Current? Could such an exploration from Africa to *The Americas* be tested in modern times? Alain Bombard was a French biologist, physician and politician famous for sailing in a small boat across the Atlantic Ocean without provision. He theorized that a human being could very well survive the trip across the ocean without provisions and decided to test his theory himself. On October 19, 1952 Bombard began his solitary trip from Tangier, Algeria, sailing in an inflatable boat. Bombard reached Barbados December 23, 1952, after 2,700 miles (4,400 kilometres) of travel. He published a book about his trip entitled *Naufragé Volontaire* in 1953. Bombard's claim was later tested by Hannes Lindemann, a German physician, navigator, and sailing pioneer. He made two solo transatlantic crossings, one in a sailing dugout canoe made while working in Liberia and the second in a 17-foot double folding kayak. His book *Alone at Sea* documents the trips. His kayak reached the Canary Islands, before sailing to the Caribbean. The 3,000-mile (4,800 km) crossing took him 72 days. Towards the end of that trip he encountered storms and capsized twice. Both men, Bombard and Lindemann, proved that it was possible to travel from Africa to The Americas in ancient times. They did it in modern times merely with boats.

Another adventurer was Thor Heyerdahl, who in 1969 and 1970 assembled a team to build a boat from papyrus and set out to prove whether the boat could cross the Atlantic from Morocco to the Caribbean. Heyerdahl based his vessel on drawings and models of ancient Egypt, and constructed the boat with builders from Lake Chad. In 1969, Heyerdahl was able to get within 160 kilometers of the Caribbean Islands, but had to abandon because the boat took on water, due to failure in attaching a tether to assist the stern, which was the method done with Egyptian boatbuilding. In 1970, he sailed off again from Morocco and this time successfully arrived at Barbados by sailing with the Canary Current.

So yes, it was not impossible for Africans to have explored the Americas and the Caribbean. Additionally, the Olmec heads in Mexico tell loudly that Africans likely arrived there. How could inhabitants carve faces of someone they had never seen? The only logical explanation is that ancient Africans undoubtedly explored the Americas and Caribbean region, whether they were Africans from

Africa, Asia, or the islands. Either African sculptors carved the stone heads or the inhabitants did, creating those faces based on Africans they had encountered and observed.

We know what happened after Columbus "*discovered*" America – death, disease, looting, and the horrific Atlantic Slave Trade. But before we discuss that tragic chapter in our history – which is still impacting real lives today - let us now examine the East African Slave Trade, and what impact it had on the world.

# CHAPTER FIVE

# The East African Slave Trade and White Slavery

SLAVERY GOES BACK TO THE beginning of mankind. The Babylonian Empire of the 21st Century BCE developed the practice of turning captured losers in warfare into slaves and deporting them to colonies and provinces under their domain. For example, Babylon deported thousands of Jewish Hebrews to "Cush" (Ethiopia) after the defeat of Judah in 607 BCE. But when did *Slave Trading* begin?

The Vikings who settled in Russia were running a slave trade route in the 9th Century. Joseph the son of Jacob was sold to a caravan of Ishmaelites by his jealous brothers for twenty pieces of silver in the year 1750 BCE. The Ishmaelites, who took Joseph to Egypt and sold him to the Chief of the bodyguards to Pharoah, were descendants of Ishmael the son of Abraham and Hagar the Egyptian, who became the surrogate wife of Abraham when his first wife Sarah could not conceive. The ancient city Opone was exporting slaves to Egypt in the 1st Century. The ancient cities Opone and Azania are attested in *The Periplus of the Erythraean Sea*:

"There is another market-town called **Opone**, into which the same things are imported as those already mentioned, and in it the greatest quantity of cinnamon is produced, (the arebo and moto), and slaves of the better sort, which are brought to Egypt in increasing numbers and a great quantity of tortoise-shell, better than that found elsewhere…The voyage to all these far-side market-towns is made from Egypt about the month of July, that is Epiphi…Beyond **Opone**, the shore trending more toward the south, first there are the small and great bluffs of **Azania**; this coast is destitute of harbors, but there are places where ships can lie at anchor, the shore being abrupt."

### TRAVEL AND TRADE IN THE INDIAN OCEAN BY A MERCHANT OF THE FIRST CENTURY"

Opone was a trade city in the area of modern-day Somalia. Azania was a region stretching from Kenya to Tanzania. Another town along the coast of East Africa was the island city Zanzibar, which was conducting international trade relations with Iran and China. The cuisine of Tanzania and Zanzibar include the traditional dishes of Biriyani, Pilau, and *Mishkani*, a barbeque dish of several meats.

Most everyone when asked, knows about the horrific Atlantic Slave Trade, also called the African Holocaust, one of the darkest sins committed on mankind, when millions of people whose birthplace was Africa were kidnapped, sold, and shipped to the Americas to be sold again and forced into a life of Slavery. The aboriginal peoples of the Americas were also oppressed, many who were forced to be slaves (See Chapter Seven). Yes, slavery goes back to mankind's beginning. An African proverb from Uganda says: "*Whoever suggested that Rats shall become our chiefs?*" But how many are knowledgeable of the *East* African Slave Trade, also called the Indian Ocean Slave Trade and the Oriental Slave Trade.

Although Africans had already migrated to South and East Asia millenniums before the slave trade began (as discussed in the previous chapter), the first Africans enslaved and sent to the Indus Valley occurred at least by 628 from Zanj, East Africa to India. The East

African Slave Trade included not only slavery in Africa, but also in the Middle East, East Asia, the Mediterranean, and European slaves. Just like the American Domestic Slave Trade had primary slave markets such as – Charleston, Boston, Richmond, New Orleans, Mobile, Memphis – the Slave Trade of East Africa had markets too – China, Iran, Saudi Arabia, India, Zanzibar, Morroco, Algiers, Tripoli, Cairo, and other destinations. Between 869 and 883, several slave revolts called the Zanj Rebellion, broke out in Iraq near Basra among those who had been sold and traded there from Zanj and other regions. The uprising was said to have involved 500,000 slaves, caused by harsh treatment from their masters and working conditions. Those enslaved were employed in harsh working conditions in sugar cane fields, salt mines, and hard labor in clearing / preparing large tracts of land. Culinary dishes of Iraq today include *Bamia*, stewed meat with okra; *Masgouf* grilled fish with olive oil; *Quzi*, whole lamb roast with rice, vegetables, nuts, and spices. Dishes from Iran passed down through generations include *Khoresht Gheimeh*, a beef and split pea stew cooked in a tomato base and served with fried potatoes. Another dish is *Fesenjan*, a combination of duck or chicken, pomegranate paste, and walnuts. Those enslaved from the Zanj region and sent to India and the Persian Gulf were also used as manual labor on ships. Many of them were also trained to be used as elite soldiers.

Beginning around the 8th century – soon after the Arab conquest of Iberia – North Africa became the center of Arab-Muslim-Berber slave raids. By the 15th century, the slave markets of Algiers, Tunis, and Tripoli were provinces of the Turkish Ottoman Empire. During this time, North Africa's involvement in the slave trade exploded. The majority of those enslaved due to Africa's North Coast slave raids along the Mediterranean from the 15th to 19th centuries were predominantly white Europeans of Christendom's Europe. Hence, the terms "white slavery", "Barbary Slave Trade", and "Barbary Pirates" began. The etymology of the word "Barbary" resulted from the ethnic term "Berber," referring to the Berbers of North Africa.

Along the coasts of North Africa and the Mediterranean, Arab-Berber pirates raided ships for their supply of men, women, and children slaves. Many of the enslaved men would be assigned the galley work of oaring the Barbary slave vessels, which was harsh work. Some rowed for decades, chained to their rowing spot, and never setting foot on shore again. Women were often made into harems. Their children were taught Islam. Many slaves in the Barbary Slave Trade converted to Islam, including women, who did not want to be separated from their children. And the ruling class in the Barbary chiefdoms also selected slaves for their use in Tripoli, Tunis, Morocco, Algiers, and Turkey. The Spanish writer Miguel de Cervantes, author of *Don Quixote*, was made a Barbary slave when he was captured in 1575 during battle in the Mediterranean, and was taken to Algiers. After five years, Cervantes was able to gain his freedom after ransom had been paid.

The majority of those kidnapped and sucked into the slavery pipeline were white Europeans. The "Barbary pirates" conducted raids in seaport towns in Italy, Spain, France, the Netherlands, Iceland, Scotland, and in England. For example, along the western coast of England were several documented slave raids. In 1631, almost the entire village of Baltimore, Ireland were rounded up and taken away on Barbary vessels. Coastal villages in Devon and Cornwall were also attacked. In April 1641, one hundred twenty passengers on the vessel *John Filmer* were captured in a slave raid when attempting to cross the Irish Sea from County Cork to England. Slave raids were so frequent at times in England, a fear that it would threaten the fishing industry was real, as fishermen were fearful their families would be kidnapped while they were away at sea. Some of those enslaved Europeans were also held ransom. It has been reported that an estimated one million and more White slaves from Europe, at least, were victims of the Barbary Slave Trade, which was a part of the entire East Coast Slave Trade.

During the 17ᵗʰ Century, the "Barbary Pirates" began attacking British ships traveling up the Coast of North Africa. Then later, during the American Revolutionary War (1775 – 1783) American merchant ships began to be attacked. Upon the ending of the Revolutionary War, the new nation, calling itself "the United States of America" had signed treaties with the Ottoman Barbary states, allowing America to pay them annual tribute in exchange for 'free from attack' passage through their waters. However, when Thomas Jefferson became the third American President, he refused to pay tribute, and sent a bombing naval fleet to the Mediterranean in May 1801 against the Barbary States of Tripoli, Algiers, and Tunis. The US Marines were also sent, which explains a verse in their hymn, "to the shores of Tripoli." During this war, one American ship named *Philadelphia* ran aground and was captured in October 1803. All of that crew were taken and sold into slavery. After a series of battles, the war involving the United States ended in 1815. This was followed by the British bombardment of Algiers in 1816 and 1824, the invasion of Algiers by France in 1830, the invasion of Tunis by France in 1881, and Tripoli under the control of Italy in 1911. But neither of these wars ended the Barbary Slave Trade. That slave trade, along with the East Coast Slave Trade, would persist. Tragically, slavery continues to persist even today.

But now, what are the origins of the indigenous peoples of the ancient Americas? And what has DNA been able to uncover?

# CHAPTER SIX

# Ancestry of the Indigenous in the Caribbean, Haiti, and the Americas

IN 2016, A RETIRED MAN living in the Pacific Northwestern part of the United States took his DNA test. Finally, his test results came back. The man was surprised to learn from the testing company that part of his DNA matched a tribal people from Siberia, known as the *Yakuts*. The man had no knowledge of this aboriginal tribe being in his ancestry, nor did his family. What was more surprising, the man was African American. He and his parents were from Kansas. His grandparents, former slaves – from Mississippi and Missouri. How did the DNA of the Yakut tribe of Siberia match an African American in the United States?

While researchers, anthropologists, and archaeologists today continue to have ongoing studies about the aboriginal peoples who first populated the Americas and present-day United States, the break-through results of DNA testing has already told us much, and has answered our basic questions of who, how, and when. Migrations came from Asia, through Siberia into Alaska, and from there into Canada and the Americas.

A skeleton of a teenage girl was found in 2007 in Mexico's Yucatan Peninsula. DNA was extracted and results of the test revealed her lineage went back to an origin in East Asia. The DNA also matched the DNA of the modern native population of the area. Subsequent genetic testings confirm that migration trail. This is not to say that the Siberia trail was the only migration path. There may have been other trails. DNA has simply confirmed this migration route at present. And on this route were many migrations of people.

Siberia – today part of Russia, but prior to them the region was home to the Huns, the Mongol Empire, and to various nomad indigenous. The annual average temperature of Siberia is about 23 degrees fahrenhit (-23 celsius) with an average of −13 f ( -25 celsius) in January and 63 f (+17 celsius) in July. The summer months are short, and long cold winters. Siberia has the largest forests. Timber has been readily available for thousands of years in the region. Food sources include fishing, and agriculture more in the southwest region. Indigenous peoples include the Buryats, Yakuts, Altai, Chukchis, Kets, Evenks, Koryaks, Kupiks, and Yukaghirs. One traditional culinary dish is Siberian *pelmeni*, made of various meats such as beef, pork, rabbit or bear, cooked in a pot with bone broth and liver. It can also be served as dumplings mixed with milk, onion, and garlic. One's appetite may also turn to Omul fish, which can be boiled, fried, or salted and smoked. An appetizer with vodka. Venison is also served, prepared in soups, dried, or fried in cowberry sauce.

How could a migration of indigenous Asian peoples of Siberia cross into Alaska, divided by the frigid waters of the Chukchi and Bering Seas? They would have frozen to death trying to cross. However, there is a landmass corridor called Beringia that connects the two continents. The ice sheets in Siberia and Alaska had lowered the water sea level by more than 100 meters and exposing the land bridge, allowing a steady stream of people to explore a new world. The Athabaskan, the Arawakan, the Carib, and the Quechuan passed through. The ancestors to the Mexica peoples, the Chickahominy peoples, the Tuscarora peoples, and many other indigenous family clans in the Americas passed through the trail across the Bering Strait. Some groups stayed in Alaska. Others stretched across Canada. Many others headed further south to South America, the Caribbean, and North America, settling the areas of present-day United States, from the west coasts of Washington, Oregon, California to the east coasts, including Virginia, the Carolinas, and the Mississippian Culture regions.

The oldest – known aboriginal civilization in the Americas, according to most current researchers at this time, is known as the Norte Chico Civilization, a society in the area of present-day Peru, and dating from around 3700 BCE. Their city at Huaricanga, located in the Fortaleza Valley on Peru's north central coast and 14 miles inland from the Pacific Ocean, was built around 3500 BCE and considered the oldest city in the Americas. Radiocarbon testing in the 1990's suggests that around 2500 BCE, the population shifted from the coast to inland sites. Their language was Athabaskan. Another Athabaskan – speaking people were the *Na-Dene*. They were ancestors of the Navaho and Apache peoples.

The ancient *Mapuche* culture in present-day Chile and Argentina in South America existed as early as 600 to 500 BCE. They are recorded in history as having resisted the Inca conquest. However, the Inca Empire of the 15th century were preceded by the empires of the *Tiwanaku* (circa 300 – 1100 CE) and the *Wari* (circa 600 – 1100 CE), both Andean cultures.

The indigenous of South America were also the first inhabitants of the Caribbean and *Haiti*, the name Columbus tried to change to La Isla Espanola, which in time corrupted to *Hispaniola*. Columbus in his journal called the indigenous people of the Bahamas *indios* (Indian) because he was searching for a pathway to India and thought he had discovered it. Before the Spanish arrived, the Taino, the Ciboney, and the Guanahatabey peoples inhabited those regions. The *Taino* (men of the good), spoke Arawakan. They also believed that inheritance rights were descended through a matrilineal line. Some researchers are divided as to where in South America the Taino had originated before their migration to the Caribbean. Some say they left Guyana and Venezuala before coming to the Caribbean and *Haiti,* which is called in Haitian Creole *Ispayola.* Other researchers believe they came from the Andes region. The Taino later migrated to Cuba by around the third century CE. A favorite eating dish of Taino origin in Cuba is Pepperpot, a spicy stew of meat, vegetables, and chili peppers. The Columbia coast and Guyana have a similar stew as well. The Ciboney were also indigenous to Cuba, Jamaica, and Haiti. They were related to Taino but had a different dialect and culture. The Guanahatabey people were also in Cuba at an early period. All three groups were present in Cuba during the arrival of Columbus.

The *Lukku – Cairi* (people of the islands) were the earliest known indigenous of *Guanahani* (the Bahamas), around 700 CE. The Lukku – Cairi (also called the Lucayans) were relatives to the Taino Arawak of Cuba, Jamaica, Haiti, and Puerto Rico. Another dish in Cuba for one's appetite is *Ropa Vieja*, a stew of shredded beef, tomato sauce, and onions with yellow rice and beer. Much of the food menu in Cuba, Haiti, Jamaica, and Puerto Rico originated with Taino Arawak, Spanish, and African influences. Some traditional dishes in Haiti are *Kibi*, a spicy meat appetizer of beef or lamb; *Griot* (fried pork); and meat and crab served with *Lalo Legume*, a mixture of jute leaves, beans, and rice, or cornmeal. The style of cooking meat called *Jerk* originated with the Taino of Jamaica.

Another early aboriginal settlement is found across the Mississippi River from St. Louis, Missouri. The site is an ancient city called Cahokia, which contains about 80 mounds in an area covering about 3.5 square miles. The city existed around 600 CE and was much larger with 120 manmade mounds. Archaeology revealed that after the year 1050, the population of the city grew to a peak of 40,000. It is the largest aboriginal site found outside of Mexico in the United States. What is even just as interesting is the fact that this same site was occupied by an *earlier* aboriginal people around 1200 BCE, but the site was later abandoned. The site today is named the Cahokia Mounds State Historic Site, in St. Clair County, Illinois. The region around St. Louis, Missouri was once part of French Louisiana under Napoleon. But millenniums before that event occurred, Louisiana held many indigenous cultures, including a site dating back to 2200 BCE and found at the Poverty Point State Historical Site in Louisiana. And another preserved archaeological site is found near Clovis, New Mexico. History recalls the enslaved African Berber from Morocco named Estevanico, also known as Esteban the Moor, who described the aboriginal peoples he met and lived with while in New Mexico. In 1528, Esteban was one of only four survivors out of 242 men from Spaniard Cabeza de Vaca's expedition in Tampa Bay, Florida. Esteban and the other men marched on foot for several months through present-day Florida, Texas, and New Mexico. Upon the four men surviving and reaching Mexico City, Esteban reported seeing aboriginal peoples in the area of present-day New Mexico.

It should be said here too, that legends of a global flood are also found among various indigenous people of the Americas, just as it is found in Africa, Asia, Europe, and the ocean islands. How is that? The Incas have several legends of a flood that surrounded the whole earth. One version is that some individuals survived a world flood by hiding on a very high mountain and repopulated the earth. The Maya of Central America's Yucatan Peninsula have an ancient belief that a great rain serpent destroyed the world by rain.

The ancient Maya people of southern Mexico and Central America built *Chichen Itza*, a large ancient city around 900 CE. They began building pyramids, according to evidence, about 3,000 years ago beginning about 1000 BCE. One of them, the Castillo of Kukulcan, had four stairways with 91 steps each, which combined with the single step at the temple entrance, equaled 365 steps, and represented the 365 days of their calendar year, in connection to the sunrises and sunsets of the planetary sun. These pyramids were also constructed for ceremonial religious purposes, as Maya's ancient rulers were also buried inside. The largest Maya pyramid in the world by volume is called *Cholula*, located in the Mexican state of Puebla. Seventy miles away from Mexico City is the ancient city of Tula, where are found two more pyramids. Ancient Tula had up to a population of 40,000 people. There are well over thirty pyramid temples in Mexico. The Mayans, or their ancestors, brought their knowledge of construction and astronomy with them, as they crossed from Asia to Alaska. And perhaps across other migration trails too, in ancient times.

There are two more documented cities to be mentioned. The Mexica, a Nahua people who themselves descended from the Chichimec peoples, built one of the largest cities in the world in 1325 CE and called it *Tenochtitlan*. The city's population was 200,000. Later in time it would become known as Mexico City. A second noted city was *Cofitachequi*, a city chiefdom located near present-day Camden, South Carolina around 1300 CE. Contemporary indigenous in that area of South Carolina were Siouan and Iroquoian tribes, such as the *Skarure* and others (which will be discussed in Chapter Seven). Like other indigenous chiefdoms of its time, Cofitachequi was the central city, with nearby mounds and smaller tribal towns within the main city's boundaries. Cofitachequi was occupied by Hernando de Soto in 1540. Sometime between 1672 and 1701, the city had been abandoned.

The Chickasaw and Choctaw peoples came to birth in the Mississippi Valley region many years before they were documented in 1540. Their seasonal migrations stretched as far as Kentucky, Tennessee, and Alabama. There is an ancient tribal tradition that Chickasaw and Choctaw were originally one people. According to the account, there were two brothers, Minko' Chiksa' and Minko' Chahta. They and their people believed in a Creator above the clouds who created all things and could be sought for guidance and direction. One day the Creator was sought help in making a decision on moving East, in the direction of the rising sun, to a new region of land. The people traveled several sunrises in two groups until reaching the Mississippi River, and upon crossing it, they stopped and rested for several days. The two groups were led by the two brothers - Chiksa' and Chahta. Finally the people were rested. The group headed by Chiksa' wanted to continue heading east. However, the group headed by Chahta wanted to settle in the area they were at. And so the people split into two nations – Chickasaw and Choctaw.

The aboriginal Cherokee who originally inhabited southwestern North Carolina, southeast Tennessee, and parts of South Carolina, Georgia, and Alabama have always claimed that the original Cherokee settlement was called *Kituwa* on the Tuckasegee River in North Carolina. In 1825, New Town, Georgia became the capital of the Cherokee Nation, and was renamed New Echota. The ancestors of the Cherokee were the Connestee people, who settled in the area later called North Carolina around 200 CE. Archeologists discovered an ancient mound of the Connestee on the site of Biltmore Estate, a national historic landmark located in Ashville, North Carolina. Other Connestee sites have also been uncovered in the state.

The *Kauwets'aka* (people of the water) is another tribe who inhabited areas in North Carolina. Known also as the Meherrin

Nation, this indigenous Iroquoian-speaking tribe first inhabited the Piedmont region of Virginia. But in the 18th century they migrated to North Carolina to separate themselves from the English colonists who were invading their ancestral lands.

In Virginia, the Powhatan Confederacy inhabited the Tidewater region. During the late 1500's, the Powhatan named Wahunsenacawh was chief to over thirty tribes. There were six original tribes – Powhatan, Arrohateck, Appamattuck, Pamunkey, Mattaponi, and Chiskiack. Their native homeland was called *Tsenacommacah* (densely inhabited land). In 1618, Wahunsenacawh died, and his younger brother Opechancanough succeeded him. Another aligned tribe of the Powhatan Confederacy were the *Chickahominy* (the coarse ground corn people). Their original territorial lands were along the Chickahominy River near Jamestown. In 1607, the Chickahominy helped the Jamestown colonists survive the winters by trading food to them, and also helped educate the colonists on how to grow their crops. But sadly, the Chickahominy began to have conflicts with the English colonists, who soon began pushing the indigenous off their lands, and passing slavery laws against them and other aboriginal peoples in Virginia (See Chapter Seven). Before the arrival of the Europeans, the aboriginal peoples of earlier times were settled in every part of present-day United States. The varied culinary tastes of Indigenous foods have found their way to our current times. Buffalo stew, from the Lakota and Cherokee peoples. Salmon dishes from the Columbia River on the West coast, serving chinook, coho, steelhead, and sockeye, originating from the Nez Perce, Umatilla, and Warm Springs tribes. Cornbread from the Powhatan and the Lenape, the Canarsie, and the Wecquaesgeek, who were the inhabitants of lower New York and Manhattan Island. Later in time, slavery would be established there in 1626. We will discuss that soon.

Modern genetic science, involving DNA samplings from indigenous descendants, has been able to identify four maternal haplogroups – A, B, C, and D – and two Y-DNA haplogroups – Q-M242 and R1. The popularity of genetic Genealogy today has exploded, with millions of people discovering Native American ancestry in their genes, and many wanting to connect and explore those aboriginal roots. For many, it is a long and rewarding journey to document such roots, but for others it is a struggle – as slavery, genocidal war, and racism have made it difficult to document their family existence. Some experience roadblocks in just simply being able to establish their own ancestral identity.

How did this come about? How did the slavery laws affect the indigenous peoples of the Americas? How did the slavery laws in North America start? How were indigenous people and people of African descent able to survive during colonial America?

# CHAPTER SEVEN

# The Enslavement of the Caribbean, Haiti, and The Americas

ON 18 JUNE 1452, THE head of the Roman Catholic Church at that time, heir and vestige of the splintered Roman Empire, Pope Nicholas V issued a Papal Bull entitled *Dum Diversas*. One can say that this issued order marked the beginning of the Roman Catholic Church's sanction and later contributor to the Atlantic Slave Trade. Being the remnant of Roman Emperor cult worship, the Roman Catholic Church had proclaimed a Holy Roman Empire, and pimping herself out to European monarchs and kings to manipulate them and make profit. Pope Nicholas V's *Dum Diversas* granted Portugal the "right" to subdue all "pagans" to "perpetual servitude." Pope Nicholas V issued another Papal Bull on 8 January 1455, *Romanus Pontifex*, reaffirming his earlier grant to Portugal, and specifically addressing the King of the Portuguese Crown, Afonso V (Alphonso V) with these words:

"We weighing all and singular the premises with due meditation, and noting that since we had formerly by other letters of ours granted among other things free and ample faculty to the aforesaid King Alfonso – to invade, search out, capture, vanquish, and subdue all Saracens and pagans whatsoever, and other enemies of Christ wheresoever placed, and the kingdoms, dukedoms, principalities, dominions, possessions, and all movable and immovable goods what-soever held and possessed by them and to reduce their persons to perpetual slavery, and to apply and appropriate to himself and his successors the kingdoms, dukedoms, counties, principalities, domin-ions, possessions, and goods, and to convert them to his and their use and profit…"

**Afonso V** in 1469, moved by the power and backing handed him from the pope, granted permission to explore the West coast of Africa. In 1482, Fernao Gomes, commissioned by Portuguese King Afonso V, set up a trading post in a long established indigenous gulf-trading area in Ghana. Gomes called his trading post *El Mina*, lo-cated in the Gulf of Guinea, which today extends to Liberia, Ivory Coast, Ghana, Togo, Benin, Nigeria, Cameroon, Equatorial Guinea, Gabon, Sao Tome and Principe, Congo, and Angola.

The king and queen of Spain, Ferdinand II and Isabella I, com-missioned the exploration of Columbus. Soon after Columbus re-turned and presented his report about the lucrative potential wealth of the Americas to the Spanish Crown, Pope Alexander VI issued two Papal Bulls on 3 May 1493, granting the Monarchy of Spain the same permissions and favors as Portugal to poach and raid West and Central Africa – and subdue humans they chose to perpetual slavery. The Spaniards left behind by Columbus in the "New World" built a fort in Haiti. Soon they began enslaving the indigenous people. Some were even sent to Spain as slaves. The Taino people and other indig-enous experienced a great loss of life due to slavery and European diseases, such as smallpox, measles, and influenza. Many of the sur-viving Indigenous escaped into the mountainous regions.

Eight years later – on 16 September 1501 – King Ferdinand II and Queen Isabella of Spain sent a letter to Nicholas Ovando, the governor of Spanish Haiti:

"Because with great care we have procured the conversion of the Indians to our Holy Catholic Faith, and furthermore, if there are still people there who are doubtful of the faith in their own conversions, it would be a hindrance, and therefore we will not permit, nor allow to go there Moors, nor Jews nor heretics nor reconciled heretics, nor persons who are recently converted to our faith, except if they are black slaves, or other slaves, that have been born under the dominion of our natural Christian subjects."

The first enslaved Africans arriving to Haiti and Brazil were sent there from Spain between 1501 – 1505. They were immediately sent to slave in the gold and copper mines. In 1511, the Spaniards, who by now were in control of Haiti and maximizing Native and African slave labor, set out to colonize Cuba. According to legend, a Taino chief in Haiti named Hatuey arrived at Cuba with four hundred of his tribe in canoes, and quickly warned some of the Indigenous on the island that the Spaniards were coming. Exactly as Hatuey had warned, the Spaniards arrived. On February 2, 1512, the Spaniards captured Hatuey and he was executed. Before his death, Hatuey was reported to have said the following:

"Here is the God the Spaniards worship. For these they fight and kill; for these they persecute us and that is why we have to throw them into the sea…They tell us, these tyrants, that they adore a God of peace and equality, and yet they usurp our land and make us their slaves…they rob our belongings, seduce our women, violate our daughters. Incapable of matching us in valor, these cowards cover themselves with iron that our weapons cannot break…"

In 1516, Pope Leo X bestowed his papal coronation upon Charles V as the new Holy Roman Emperor and monarch of Spain, and Archduke of Austria. Charles was the grandson of Maximilian I, former holy roman emperor. Charles's wife was Isabella of Portugal, the granddaughter of Ferdinand and Isabella. Two years after his coronation, Charles V granted a charter on 18 August 1518 for permission to transport 4,000 enslaved people directly from the continent of Africa to Haiti, Cuba, and Puerto Rico. Prior to this, enslaved Africans had been transported to the Caribbean from Spain. But now, Charles V commanded the enslaved of Africa go directly to the "Spanish new world." His charter said in part:

"Our officials who reside in the city of Seville in our House of Trade of the Indies; know ye that I have given permission, and by the present instrument do give it, to Lorenzo de Gorrevod, governor of Bresa, member of my Council, whereby he, or the person or persons who may have his authority therefore, may proceed to take to the Indies, the islands and the mainland of the ocean sea already discovered or to be discovered, four thousand Negro slaves both male and female, provided that they be Christians, in whatever proportions he may choose…should make any arrangements with traders or other persons to ship the said slaves, male or female, direct from the isles of Guinea and other regions…"

In 1519, one year after the so-called "Charter" was granted, enslaved Africans began arriving in New Spain (Spanish Mexico). Then in 1523, three hundred enslaved Africans were imported into Cuba. The first enslaved Africans arriving at La Florida was in late 1526, as a significant part of the expedition of Lucas Vazquez de Ayllon, who brought as many as 100 enslaved. Earlier in 1521, Vazquez de Ayllon made landfall at Winyah Bay, South Carolina and seized seventy indigenous persons to be taken to Haiti as slave labor. But in less than two months this time in 1526, his settlement in La Florida was abandoned due to disease, mutiny, and an African rebellion burning down the house to one of the leaders. Legend claims the Africans ran off and joined with the local aboriginal Guale tribe. Other expeditions followed, including the expedition of Spanish admiral Pedro Menendez de Aviles, who arrived at La Florida and founded St. Augustine on 8 September 1565, bringing in more enslaved Africans. By the end of the 16th century, there were perhaps fifty enslaved Africans at St. Augustine, including a woman named Gratia, who gave birth to an infant boy on 5 January 1595 and named Esteban.

As the Spanish accelerated the Atlantic Slave Trade, the Portuguese continued their involvement as well, enlarging their operations and growing demand to purchase Africans in the Congo and Angola. The Portuguese also developed large-scale slave trading with Japan, as hundreds of Japanese men and women were being purchased. Some Japanese enslaved were found in South America and Mexico. This was due to a slave trade route established from Manila to Acapulco. Three Japanese slaves were documented in Mexico in the 16th century – Gaspar Fernandes, Miguel, and Ventura. Miguel was sold by a Portuguese slave trader in Manila in 1594. Gaspar Fernandes was sold in Japan as an eight-year old in 1585.

By May 1607, the colony of Jamestown was founded on the coast of Virginia, but on the land of Wahunsunacawh, the head of the Powhatans. Hostilities arose between the Powhatans and the colonists during 1609 – 1614, until a peace treaty was formed with the marriage of Pocahontas to colonist John Rolfe.

In Africa, the Portuguese military campaign of 1618 marched on into neighboring Ndongo ally Matamba and pillaged them, with the help of the mercenary Imbangala (See the book *1619 – Twenty Africans*, by the author). Thousands in Matamba and Ndongo were killed and many more taken as slaves, as the war spilled into the year 1619. The prisoners were made slaves and taken to the slave port of Luanda in Portuguese Angola. There, the slaves would be baptized, loaded onto slave ships, and sent to Brazil and Vera Cruz, New Spain (Mexico).

In August 1619, the Spanish slave ship *San Juan Bautista* left Luanda with 350 enslaved Africans heading to Vera Cruz, Mexico. Towards the end of August, the ship having crossed the Atlantic and nearing the coast of Campeche, two English vessels attacked it. One of the privateer ships was called *Treasurer*. The other was called *White Lion*. They stole off of *Bautista* about 50 enslaved Africans, who had been captured in the Portuguese wars. According to historian Engel Sluiter, Spanish records indicated that on August 30, 1619, *Bautista* ended up delivering to Vera Cruz only 147 kidnapped enslaved out of a shipment of 350, and that it had been robbed by two "corsairs".

Both the *Treasurer* and *White Lion* immediately set sail to Jamestown to see if the colony would engage in a trade transaction involving the 50 persons shackled on their vessels. The ship *White Lion* arrived at Point Comfort (now Hampton), and according to John Rolfe, the secretary of the Virginia colony, offered "20, and odd Negroes," which were "bought for victualle…at the best and easiest rate they could" by cape merchant Abraham Peirsey, and by the governor Sir George Yeardley. So twenty-some human beings were sold for food.

About three or four days later, the other pirate ship, *Treasurer*, anchored at Point Comfort, and bringing 25 to 29 enslaved Angolans who had been seized from the Spanish ship *Bautista* bound for Vera Cruz. How this second group of 25 or more were divided is also not known, however, tobacco planter William Peirce took a woman from the group whose name was Angelo. Not all of this number may have been left in Virginia, as it had been said that the ship captain of *Treasurer* was planning to trade off some of his kidnapped group in Bermuda.

Some of the Africans had European names, as many in Ndongo and Kongo had been baptized and practiced Portuguese Catholicism. Even if their religious conversions in Ndongo and Kongo may have been more for social or political reasons, the Angolans' knowledge of Christendom would have pulled considerable weight among the Virginian colonists because, at that time in England and in Virginia, social rank in society was determined, not by Race, but by Class and Religion, "Christian" or "Heathen." But in time, sadly, that social viewpoint would eventually change.

By March 1620, a census conducted by the Virginia colonists revealed there were 32 Africans in the colony that year, 15 males and 17 females. This number may reflect the actual number of Angolans who were brought roughly six months earlier in late August 1619. Or, the number was higher and some had been transported elsewhere, or perhaps died. Disease was already a constant threat in the colony. Some of the Africans might also have been exposed to sickness prior to their arrival. Malnutrition and famine had been a constant problem in the Virginia colony in prior years.

In early 1619, Lieutenant William Peirce and Sir George Yeardley had made a treaty with the Chickahominy. But on March 22, 1622, there was an attack on the colonists by the Powhatan, led by Wehocshwah's younger brother Opechancanough. One African named Antonio, who had been brought to the colony in 1621, was working on the Edward Bennett plantation when the attack reached there. The staged uprising killed about 347 colonists along the James River plantations, including 52 at Bennett's plantation. Antonio was one of four men who managed to survive the attack. At the Flowerdew Hundred Plantation, owned by Sir George Yeardley, six persons were killed.

According to the 1624 census, 11 Africans were living at the Flowerdew Hundred plantation. Only four names are known – Anthony, William, John, and another Anthony. The woman Angelo who came in 1619 was listed as living at Lieutenant Peirce's household. Four Africans lived at the puritan Edward Bennett's plantation – Peter, Frances, Margaret, and Antonio. The next year, the

1625 muster showed 3 males and 5 females living at Yeardley's residence at Jamestown, and four men, two women, and a child living at Flowerdew Hundred. On September 19, 1625, the General Court awarded temporary custody of an African man named Brass (or Brase) to Yeardley's wife, Lady Temperance Yeardley. The court also ordered to pay forty pounds of good tobacco per month for his labor as long as Brass remained under her service, and for Captain Nathaniel Bass to provide clothing to him. Brass had come to Virginia on a ship called *Portugal* with a Captain Jones, who later sold Brass to Nathaniel Bass, whose plantation was next to the Edward Bennett plantation. The sale to Captain Nathaniel Bass was later voided. The 1625 census revealed an African named John Pedro and an African couple named Anthony and Isabella, lived in Elizabeth City that year. Anthony and Isabella also had a male infant named William.

These remaining Angolans from Ngondo and Kongo, beginning in 1619, would continue surviving Jamestown's indentured servitude, but not yet as legalized slaves, as was the case with the enslaved indigenous. That would soon change. But before we examine that time period, let us first learn what took place 742 nautical miles away from Jamestown, Virginia in the year 1626.

PLAN OF LOWER DECK WITH THE STOWAGE OF 292 SLAVES
130 OF THESE BEING STOWED UNDER THE SHELVES AS SHEWN IN FIGURE D & FIGURE 5.

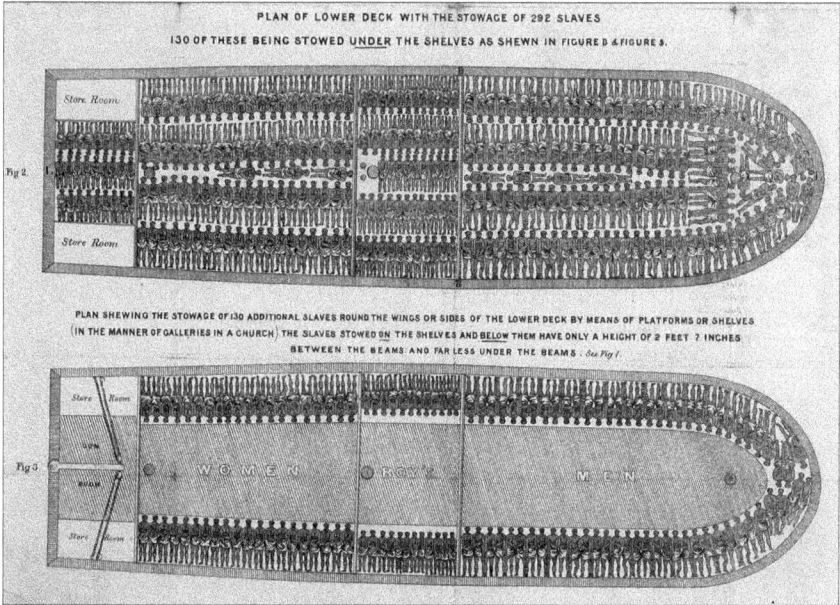

Slave Ship. The Dutch traders from the Netherlands brought the first Africans to Manhattan, New York in 1626. During the 1500's, millions of enslaved Africans were shipped to the Caribbean, Haiti, and The Americas. The Pope sanctioned the Atlantic Slave Trade by authorizing Spain and Portugal to invest in human trafficking.

NEW-YORK, 21 April 1783.

THIS is to certify to whomfoever it may concern, that the Bearer hereof

Cato Hammiay

a Negro, reforted to the Britifh Lines, in confequence of the Proclamations of Sir William Howe, and Sir Henry Clinton, late Commanders in Chief in America; and that the faid Negro has hereby his Excellency Sir Guy Carleton's Permiffion to go to Nova-Scotia, or wherever elfe He may think proper.

By Order of Brigadier General Birch,

Book of Negroes, a document containing the records of 3000 Africans in New York who were granted their freedom with the British in 1783, just as the United States of America took over New York. Many were given passage to Nova Scotia and Sierra Leone.

Harlem, New York, 1925.

The Congo (author MONUSCO photos https://commons.wikimedia.org/wiki/
File:Photo_of_the_Day_17_February_2014_(12589890963).jpg

Dred Scott, circa 1857, the time of his court
case before the Supreme Court.

Chief Joseph of the Nez Perce, and his family, circa 1880.

William Still, conductor of the Underground Railroad.

Queen Makea of the Cook Islands, being read the Annexation Proclamation of her country by the British Colonial governor of New Zealand.

Two Women on the Eskridge plantation in Roane County, Tennessee, circa 1850's. Today DNA genetic science is connecting many descendants of enslaved African and Native indigenous people, including those who lived on several Eskridge plantations spread throughout the South.

CHAPTER EIGHT

# 1626

IN THE YEAR 1626, AT an area called *Mahattoe* by the aboriginal Lenape along the east bank of the Hudson River, eleven Africans from Central Africa were unloaded onto the harbor of a Dutch colony called New Amsterdam (New York City). These Africans, all males, were Paulo Angola, Big Manuel, Little Manuel, Manuel de Gerrit de Reus, Simon Congo, Antony Portuguese, Gracia, Piter Santomee, Jan Francisco, Little Antony, and Jan Fort Orange.

The men had been originally captured by the Portuguese, held in bonds at their slave-trade port Luanda, and loaded onto a Spanish slave ship heading to the Caribbean. However, a military ship belonging to the Dutch West India Company intercepted the Spanish slaver and stole the eleven men from it, holding the men against their will yet again.

The Dutch West India Company founded their permanent colony in an area called by the Lenape *Paggank* (nut island) in 1624, which later became the area of Albany, New York The Dutch named their colony New Netherland, the colony encompassing present-day New York, New Jersey, Delaware, Connecticut, and parts of Pennsylvania and Rhode Island. Actually, in 1613, a free black trader working for a Dutch fur trading company as a translator came to Manhattan Island from the Dominican. His name was Juan Rodrigues, who stayed in Manhattan and traded with the local Lenape on the island.

The Netherlands, who broke for their independence from the Spanish branch of the House of Habsburg in 1581, established the Dutch West India Company in 1621, for the purpose of carrying on economic warfare against Spain and Portugal. The company's charter was aimed toward Dutch interests in the Atlantic Slave Trade, Brazil, the Caribbean, and North America. The Dutch West India Company was actually a continuation of the *Dutch East Indies Company*, a corporation the Netherlands founded in 1602 to champion the Dutch war of independence from Spain (one of the imperial estates of the Holy Roman Empire). More of this will be discussed in Chapter Ten.

Sometime later in the year 1626, after the eleven men from the Congo region had been brought to *Mahattoe* by the Dutch – who planned to use them for slave labor in their town New Amsterdam – the Dutch West India Company purchased 22, 000 acres – Mahattoe Island – from the Lenape people. One member of the Dutch company sent a letter to inform his government, The Netherlands, of the purchase:

"High and Mighty Lords,

Yesterday the ship the Arms of Amsterdam arrived here. It sailed from New Netherland out of the River Mauritius on the 23d of September. They report that our people are in good spirit and live in peace. The women also have borne some children there. They have purchased the Island Manhattes from the Indians for the value of 60 guilders. It is 11,000 morgens in size. They had all their grain sowed by the middle of May, and reaped by the middle of August. They sent samples of

these summer grains: wheat, rye, barley, oats, buckwheat, canary seed, beans and flax…

In Amsterdam, the 5th of November anno 1626
Your High and Mightiness's obedient, P. Schaghen"

The changing faces of the aggressors upon the real estate of the
indigenous in the Caribbean, Brazil, Haiti, Mexico, and other aboriginal homelands had now spilled over into the virgin lands along
the Atlantic East Coast. The molding of the future United States was
now in play, as Spain controlled Florida, England held Virginia, and
the Dutch Netherlands claimed New York. Eventually, Britain would
take over that institution of oppression in New York, especially in
New York City. In time, the Thirteen Colonies of the American
Revolution would take its turn to govern. Would it do any better –
allow ALL people freedom? History would answer that question in a
matter of time.

The year 1626 was indeed a marker on the history timeline, as
Africans imported into Manhattan Island, as well as the indigenous
already living there for generations, began laying the foundations for
New York City from their free slave labor. It was also the beginning
foundation for a free Black community that came into existence, before
slavery had yet to be abolished there. . In time, other kidnapped
persons would come directly from Africa, the Caribbean, Brazil, and
Curacao. In 1627, three enslaved women of color were brought to
Manhattan Island. The name of one of them was Dorothy Creole.

The eleven Africans were then put to work by the Dutch West
India Company. In time, other kidnapped persons would come di-
rectly from Africa, the Caribbean, Brazil, and Curacao. Yes, the Dutch
Netherlands had now succumbed to the thirsty grab for wealth,

power, and profit from the invaluable resource of human trafficking, by competing rivalries with Spain and Portugal.

Today, descendants of the eleven men brought in 1626 – as well as other enslaved persons of African descent who were later brought into New York – tell the stories that were passed down to them from their ancestors. The conditions and circumstances which led to a free African community emerging in New York City during Dutch rule (and later British and American rule) are documented.

The documents reveal, oddly, that even though Africans were being held against their will in the Dutch colony of New York, the Dutch style-of-rule still allowed enslaved persons their legal rights, and access to their judicial system. One example being on December 9, 1638, when Anthony the Portuguese, one of the eleven men, sued a white merchant for injury his dog caused to Anthony's hog. Anthony, a slave, was awarded damages. Another case involved Manuel de Reus, also of the eleven, who in 1639 was granted a power of attorney to collect his back wages from his employer. The colony's laws allowed enslaved Africans to legally marry, and own property, including land. They also were not prohibited from inter-racial marriage. The Dutch also made the provision for manumission, but in two phases: *conditional freedom*, and full freedom.

After serving the colony in Manhattan for eighteen years, the eleven Africans petitioned the courts for their release, claiming the Company had promised them freedom. The petition also stated their desire for liberty in order to care for their families. On February 25, 1644, the Dutch West India Company granted the men conditional freedom:

*"We, Willem Kieft, director general, and the council of New Netherland, having considered the petition of the Negroes named Paulo Angola, Big Manuel, Little Manuel, Manuel de*

*Gerrit de Reus, Simon Congo, Antony Portuguese, Gracia, Piter Santomee, Jan Francisco, Little Antony and Jan Fort Orange, who have served the Company for 18 or 19 years, that they may be released from their servitude and be made free."*

Manumission of Manuel de Gerrit et al, 25 February 1644

The Company only granted the men conditional freedom, as long as they would pay yearly dues of "30 skepels of maize, wheat, peas or beans, and one fat hog," and to assist the Company when needed, or else face being re-enslaved. The Dutch company also granted them land. Other Africans were given freedom and granted parcels of land. In 1659 and 1660, the Company Director, Stuyvesant, granted more land lots to African-descent families in Manhattan. In 1662, the Company granted conditional freedom to three women. One of the women, named Mayken, just a few months later petitioned for full freedom. Mayken was granted her full freedom, after thirty-four years of being enslaved. On September 4, 1664, a petition for full freedom was presented from eight African men and filed with the Council. On December 21, 1664, these eight men were granted full freedom: Ascento Angola, Christoffel Santome, Pieter Pietersz Criolie, Antony Antonysz Criolie, Salomon Pietersz Criolie, Jan Guinea, Lowies Guinea, and Bastiaen Pietersz.

The freed Africans and their family heirs of descent created the first free Black community in Manhattan. The records show they cared for one another, as they strived to carve out a life of existence in this new village they had to accept as their new home. Anna van Angola was granted six acres. She had been widowed twice. Sebastiaen de Britto married Isabel Kisana, who was from Angola. They received land. Anthony Fernando Portuguese found a wife in 1642. A widow named Catalina received land. She had a two year old child. Bastiaen d' Angola was given freedom in 1654. No strings were attached to his manumission, except "to gain a livelihood for himself, as any other free person may do." Willem Antonys Portuguese received land from his deceased father, Anthony Portuguese. Domingo Angola married a woman named Maycke. She later received a land grant. Manuel Trompeter's land was confirmed to his children Bernard and Christina. In 1663, Domingo Angola petitioned the Council that Manuel Trompeter's orphaned daughter Christina be granted her freedom, which was so orderd. Big Manuel's land went to his widow Christina de Angola. Paolo D'Angola's land went to his widow Dorothy Creole, one of the three women who arrived in 1627. Pieter Santome's land went to his sons Lucas and Salomon. Lucas was an apprentice in the barber trade. Little Anthony married Lucie d'Angola on May 5, 1641. They had a son, Anthony, in July 1643. However, Lucie died about four weeks later. The child Anthony was adopted by his godmother Dorothy, the wife of Paolo d'Angola. Anthony's father Little Anthony later died in 1648, and Dorothy's husband Paolo also died. In 1661, Dorothy and her new husband, Emanuel Pieters, petitioned the Council that their foster son Anthony "be declared by your noble honors to be a free person" so that "he could inherit by last will and testament." Freedom was awarded Anthony. He later received the land patent of his late father.

These families lived on their land in the town of Manhattan for generations as free people, as shown by an entry notated in the journal of Jasper Danckaerts:

"We went from the city, following the Broadway, over the _valley_, or the fresh water. Upon both sides of this way were many habitations of negroes, mulattoes and whites. These negroes were formerly the proper slaves of the (West

India) company, but, in consequence of the frequent changes and conquests of the country, **they have obtained their freedom** and settled themselves down where they have thought proper, and thus on this road, where they have ground enough to live on with their families. We left the village, called the Bowery, lying on the right hand, and went through the woods to New Harlem, a tolerably large village situated on the south side of the island..."

Journal of Jasper Danckaerts, 1679 – 1680

According to his description of the Manhattan, New York neighborhood, we can decipher the neighborhood is in present-day Greenwich Village.

The British would soon take over New York, a change of government in New Amsterdam, which would have reverberating effects on the people of color on Manhattan Island for several decades. On August 27, 1664, four military ships of war from England sailed into New Amsterdam's harbor and demanded the Dutch colony of New Netherlands to surrender. The articles of surrender were soon signed in September 1664. As the British and Dutch were preparing for official transfer of power, the Dutch Company Director, Stuyvesant, fearing that the people of color might never claim their freedom under the new British government, began freeing as many enslaved people of color as he could within days of the transfer. Land was also granted as previously discussed.

After the British took control of New York, slavery was legalized, and slave codes were put into effect. Another change was – unlike Dutch rule which allowed people of color access to the judicial system and allowed a measure of legal rights – no rights were allowed anyone who was labeled a "slave." The British did tolerate former manumissions under the Dutch, however. But any "slip of the law" for a free person of color could mean being sold back into slavery in New York. In 1711, a slave market was formally opened at the end of Wall Street, a street barricade built in 1685 which crossed the indigenous trail path later called Broadway. Wall Street also served as a marketplace where enslaved persons could be hired out by their defined-by-law owners. The next year, 1712, a revolt against slavery broke out, killing 8 whites and 25 blacks.

Slavery in New York by 1730 had become so systematic and controlling that "An Act for the more effectual preventing and punishing the conspiracy and insurrection of Negro and other slaves and for better regulating them" was passed, prohibiting an assembly of three or more people of color:

"Foresmuch as the number of slaves in the cities of New York and Albany, as also within the several couties, towns and manors within this colony doth daily increase, and that they have oftentime been guilty of confederating together in running away, and of other ill and dangerous practices, it is unlawful for above three slaves to meet together at any time, or at any other place than when it shall happen they meet in some servile employment for their masters' or mistresses' profit, and by their masters' or mistresses' consent, upon penalty of being whipt upon the naked back, at the discretion of any one justice of the piece [sic], not exceeding forty lashes"

Another ordinance was enacted in 1737, "A Law for Regulating Negro's & Slaves in the Night Time", which made it unlawful to:

"That no Negro, Mulatto or Indian Slave, shall appear in the Streets of this City, above an hour after Sun-set without a candle and Lanthorn, on penalty of being Whipt at the Publick Whipping Post."

In 1741, another revolt against slavery rose up, which lasted for six months. By 1780, during the American Revolutionary War, about

10,000 people of African descent lived in New York City. This was in part to the British announcing freedom to any enslaved persons who left their American masters and come to the British side. Thousands came. One of them was a sixteen-year-old girl named Deborah Squash, a runaway from George Washington's slaves. Another person who made their way to New York was Boston King, who had been enslaved in South Carolina before he ran away. The war ended in 1781, and negotiations began between the two governments in Paris, France, where a treaty was drafted on November 30, 1782 and signed on September 3, 1783. However, during April – September 1783, representatives of Great Britain and the United States met at a tavern in Manhattan to compile a roll of names to former enslaved persons who wished to evacuate with the British rather than remain in New York. Known as the *Book of Negroes*, the official title was also called "Inspection Roll of Negroes New York, New York City Book No. 1 April 23 – September 13, 1783." The tavern where the list was compiled – Queens Head Tavern – was owned by a free black named Samuel Fraunces. Today the tavern is located on Pearl Street in Manhattan. About 3,000 persons of British loyalists are named, of whom the United States argued for the return of their "property", but British commander Guy Carlton refused, saying it would be "A dishonorable violation of public faith" to not keep their promise to those who wished to leave New York with them. The evacuation took place on November 25, 1783. The three thousand loyalists of African descent ended up resettling in various places. Many went to Nova Scotia and the West Indies, others to London, and several to Sierra Leone, where they founded Freetown in 1792. Deborah Squash, and her husband Harvey, went to Nova Scotia. Boston King also went there, and then later to Sierra Leone.

Slavery in New York was finally abolished on July 4, 1827. It would be another thirty-eight years more of American slavery until the United States Constitution was amended and legalized slavery was abolished in the nation. But would that event mark a change inside people's hearts? Another important question – how did American Slavery occur? What really happened under the first English colony called Jamestown?

Life went on for the remaining Ndongo and Kongo Africans who had arrived in Virginia in 1619 and thereafter. Those Africans who had finished out their Indenture were pronounced free, and now able to acquire land and become property owners. Free Black women were not required to be tithed, but were kept exempt right along with the English women. Free Black men who owned land were not legally barred from buying the contracts of other indentured servants in order to provide labor for their lands. Free Africans were not barred from marrying any woman who was free to marry in the colony, regardless of race. Their children were born free, whether black, mulatto, or mestizo, and were allowed to be baptized and be recognized as "Christian." They also began calling one another "Malunga," to remember who they were.

While Queen Nzinga of Ndongo was fighting another Portuguese assault on her kingdom, the captain of a Massachusetts Bay ship *Fortune* plundered 100 enslaved Angolans from a Spanish vessel in 1628 and had them taken to Virginia to be bartered and sold, most likely at Jamestown. John Ellzey II, a successful merchant in Southampton, England, wrote to Edward Nicholas, Secretary to the Duke of Buckingham, about the "prized goods" taken by the slave ship *Fortune*:

"A frigate that came from the West India' taken by Arthur Guy, who was in command of the Fortune of London. The Fortune 'hath taken an Angola man with man[y] Negros, intended to be disposed of in the Indias but the Captain sent them to Virginia where they sould and did barter them for Tobaco which tobacco is come home in the Plantation partlie belonging unto this Towne.' Ellzey 'conceave my lord hath righte in the tobacco which was soulde for those Negroes."

The Angolans were unloaded and dispersed out to the several tobacco plantations along the James River and other county masters, to begin their time as Indentured servants. No doubt many of them were shocked but uplifted in spirit to meet a community from their language-speaking homelands already here.

The African community in the colony continued to grow, as more family alliances emerged, marriages took place and children grew up, ready to take their place in the world, receiving training in various occupation skills from their parents, grandparents, and great-grandparents. Food dishes in New York, Virginia, and the South went through a transformation, as they were fused together through African, Native Indigenous, and European ingredients and cooking methods. The art of deep-frying was known by Africans who were brought to North America, and also used by the Native Indigenous, as fried chicken and barbeque pork are deeply embedded in the American cuisine, as are the sides – black-eyed peas, okra, rice, squash, collard greens, potatoes, hominy, grits, cornbread, fritters, hush puppies. At New York food carts, enslaved persons sold oysters, *Indian corn peaches*, and hot corn on the cob. The European colonists brought milk, eggs, flour, and sugar. In Louisiana, the French, West African, and Spanish fused a Creole cuisine in that region, which created such well-known dishes as Jambalaya, Gumbo, Crawfish etouffee, and Bananas Foster.

But the freedoms that the African communities enjoyed in the Virginia colony would soon begin to whittle away bit by bit.

# CHAPTER NINE

# Enslavement of Indigenous and Africans in Virginia and the Carolinas

IN 1639, A LAW WAS passed in the Virginia colony that Africans could no longer possess firearms:

> "ALL persons except negroes to be provided with arms and ammunition or be fined at pleasure of the Governor and Council"

That was surprising. Up until then, the statute since 1619 required everyone to attend church on the Sabbath and added:

> "and all such as bear arms shall bring their pieces, swords, powder and shot."

In fact, a person would be fined if failing to do so. The threat of attack by the indigenous tribes at that time was real. No one was to go out in the fields unarmed. Even a sentry was to be standing guard nearby. The 1619 statute was reissued again in 1632:

> "All men that are fitting to bear arms, shall bring their pieces to the church…"

But this new edict in 1639 did not just come overnight. The House of Burgesses had a reason for this new law. A thought process had been put into place. Soon, two runaway cases came before the Courts in July of 1640:

"Whereas Hugh Gwyn hath by order from this Board brought back from Maryland three servants formerly run away from the said Gwyn, the court doth therefore order that the said three servants shall receive the punishment of whipping and to have thirty stripes apiece one called Victor, a [D]utchman, the other a Scotchman called James Gregory, shall first serve out their times with their master according to their Indentures and one whole year apiece after the time of their service is Expired…the third being a Negro named John Punch shall serve his said master and his assigns for the time of his natural Life here or elsewhere"

9th, July 1640

"Whereas complaint has been made to this Board by Capt Wm Pierce Esqr that six of his servants and a negro of Mr Reginolds has plotted to run away unto the Dutch plantation from their said masters and did assay to put the same in Execution upon Saturday night being the 18th day July 1640 as appeared to the Board by Examinations of Andrew Noxe, Richd Hill, Richd Cookeson and John Williams and likewise by confession of Christopher Miller, Peter Wilcocke, and Emanuel the foresaid Negro who had at the fore said time, taken the skiff of the said Capt Wm Pierce their master, and corn powder and shot guns, to accomplish their said purposes, which said p[er]sons sailed down in the said skiff to Elizabeth river where they were taken and brought back again, the Court taking the same into consideration, as a dangerous p[re]cident for the future time did order that Christopher Miller a Dutchman should receive the punishment of whipping and to have thirty stripes, and to be burnt in the cheek with the letter R and to work with a shakle on his legg for one whole year...and after his full time of service is Expired with his said master to serve the colony for seven whole years, and the said Peter Wilcocke to receive thirty stripes and to be Burnt in the cheek with the letter R...and the said Andrew Noxe to receive thirty stripes...and Emanuel the Negro to receive thirty stripes and to be burnt in the cheek with the letter R and to work in shakle one year or more as his master shall see cause..."

22nd July, 1640

Two cases before the courts in the same month involving English and African runaway servants. The case of July 22nd does show the court's impartiality in meting out the sentences, although severe. Four of the men – Christopher, Peter, Andrew, and Emanuel – all received thirty lashes. Additionally, Emanuel "the Negro" wasn't the only person to receive a branding of the letter "R" (Runaway) to his cheek – Christopher and Peter did as well. That was a horrible form of punishment. However, the other court case of July 9th revealed the beginning of something very sinister. Something seemed different about this case. All three men also received whippings for their crime. But for Victor the Dutchman, and James Gregory the Scotchman, their added punishment for running away was merely to serve one additional year apiece after the time of their current service expired. However, for the "Negro named John Punch" his stiff sentence was:

"...serve his said master and his assigns **for the time of his natural Life here or elsewhere**"

John Punch (sometimes spelled Bunch) was sentenced to servitude for the rest of his life, and wherever he went. The ruling did not use the word "slave", but there was no question the Virginia Assembly had begun to legally define one. Another ruling was issued in 1642, aimed at the African community in the colony:

"Be it also enacted and confirmed That there be tenn pounds of tob'o. per poll & a bushell of corne per poll paid to the ministers within the severall parishes of the collony for all tithable persons, that is to say, as well for all youths of sixteen years of age as upwards, as also for all negro women at the age of sixteen years"

Now the females of African descent sixteen years and up, would be taxed.

Another peculiar case came before the courts, involving a free African, Anthony Johnson and his servant John Casor. Anthony Johnson was one of the Angolans who came in 1619. He later gained his freedom and married an African woman named Mary, who had been brought to Virginia sometime before 1623. They later moved to Northampton County, Virginia where Anthony had acquired 250 acres of land by 1651. Anthony had become so prosperous, he was able to import five indentured servants of his own. Because of this, he was granted the headrights to an additional 250 acres. A headright was a legal grant of land that the Virginia Company gave to any settler willing to pay the transportation costs for another person to be brought to Virginia. In turn, that person would become an Indentured servant in order to repay the landowner for the transportation costs. Landowners would receive 50 acres for each person brought over to expand the colony and the economy. Thus, many landowners and families grew in power by receiving large grants when they imported many servants and slaves. This also created an abuse of power, as the elite could be issued headrights of large tracts of land for fictitious people and falsifying the records. The number of headrights issued was four times more than the increase in population. The headrights system also kept many poor settlers from acquiring their own land, resulting in a sharecropper's arrangement, and strife between the rich and poor.

One of Anthony Johnson's servants was John Casor, also a person of African descent as Johnson, who said he had been imported for a seven or eight year term, and after serving that amount, claimed that Johnson would not allow his freedom. Johnson claimed that Casor did not have such a contract, but that he had Casor "for his life." Johnson let Casor go, upon the urgings of his family, and Casor went to work for another landowner named Robert Parker. Later, Johnson accused Parker of taking his worker and filed a lawsuit, *Johnson vs. Parker*. The Court made its ruling on March 8, 1654:

> "Whereas complaint was this daye made to ye court by ye humble peticion of Anth. Johnson Negro ag[ains]t Mr. Robert Parker that hee detayneth one John Casor a Negro the plaintiffs Serv[an]t under pretense yt the sd Jno. Casor is a freeman the court seriously considering & maturely weighing ye premises doe fynd that ye sd Mr. Robert Parker most unrightly keepeth ye sd Negro John Casor from his r[igh]t mayster Anth. Johnson as it appeareth by ye Deposition of Capt. Samll Gold smith & many probable circumstances. be it therefore ye Judgement of ye court & ordered that ye sd Jno. Casor negro, shall forthwith bee turned into ye service

of his sd master Anthony Johnson and that the sd Mr. Robert Parker make payment of all charges in the suite and execution"

The Court did not grant Casor his freedom, but ruled that he be returned to the service of his master Anthony Johnson. The court, in effect, agreed with Johnson that Casor was his servant "for his life." Of course, Johnson could at any time release Casor from servitude and grant him freedom. But the point was, the court had given judicial sanction to the right of a "Negro" to own slaves of his own race for life. Thus, the courts were still perfecting and creating a legal basis and precedent for a lifetime servant or slave.

Then, in 1662, the word "slave" was used for the first time in Virginia law pertaining to persons of African descent in the colony:

"WHEREAS some doubts have arrisen whether children got by any Englishman upon a negro woman should be **slave** or ffree, Be it therefore enacted and declared by this present grand assembly, that all children borne in this country shall be held bond or free only according to the condition of the mother, And that if any christian shall committ ffornication with a negro man or woman, hee or shee soe offending shall pay double the ffines imposed by the former act."

This statute began to legally define and slowly create a new status in Virginian life – the slave. Any children born in the colony moving forward, would be either free or held bound, meaning slave, according to the condition of the mother. So if the mother was defined a slave, so would the child. This was totally contrary to English law. The Virginia colony followed English primogeniture law, generally defined as birth lineage by paternal acknowledgement, the father.

But this statute circumvented that, transferring any entitlement to the legal status of the mother. Only if the mother was free, could the child be.

By this time of the 1640's, England had entered the Atlantic Slave Trade, with its keen interest in Barbados and the sugar production in the Caribbean. London opened a slave port in 1660. That same year, the Virginia Assembly passed a statute in the colony entitled *"An Act for the Dutch and all other Strangers for Tradeing to this Place."* The Royal Crown, aiming to strengthen England's international commerce, prohibited Dutch ships from trading to the colony. However, this Virginia statute did not prohibit Virginia planters to trade tobacco to the Dutch in exchange for "negro slaves."

Virginia had clearly shifted in its attitude and viewpoint towards the Free Africans and Indentured servants of color within the colony. Other statutes were passed to further cripple and define them. In 1667 was passed *"An act declaring that baptisme of slaves doth not exempt them from bondage*:

> "WHEREAS some doubts have risen whether children that are slaves by birth, and by the charity and piety of their owners made pertakers of the blessed sacrament of baptisme, should by vertue of their baptisme be made ffree; It is enacted and declared by this grand assembly, and the authority thereof, that the conferring of baptisme doth not alter the condition of the person as to his bondage or ffreedome; that diverse masters, ffreed from this doubt, may more carefully endeavour the propagation of christianity by permitting children, though slaves, or those of greater growth if capable to be admitted to that sacrament"

The House of Burgesses decided that slaves born in Virginia would not become free even if they were baptized, as had been the custom before. In 1670 another statute passed, called *"Noe Negroes nor Indians to buy christian servants"* Act:

> "WHEREAS it hath beene questioned whither Indians or negroes manumited, or otherwise free, could be capable of purchasing christian servants, It is enacted that noe negroe or Indian though baptised and enjoyned their owne ffreedome shall be capable of any such purchase of christians, but yet not debarred from buying any of their owne nation"

The wording of this statute implied that prior to its issuance, "Negroes" and "Indians" *could* purchase persons of *any nationality* within the colony for service. Otherwise, there would have been no point in passing the ruling. The statute also made it clear that "Christian servants" in the colony no longer included "Negroes" or "Indians", even if they were baptized. The final four rulings between 1670 – 1705 would put the final nail in the coffin, and produce the desired result for chattel slavery. In 1672 came the *Act for the apprehension and suppression of runaways, negroes, and slaves*:

> "FORASMUCH as it hath beene manifested to this grand assembly that many negroes have lately beene, and now are out in rebellion in sundry parts of this country, and that noe meanes have yet beene found for the apprehension and suppression of them from whome many mischeifes of very dangerous consequence may arise to the country if either other negroes, Indians or servants should happen to fly forth and joyne with them; for the prevention of which, be it enacted by the governour, councell and burgesses of this grand assembly,

**and by the authority thereof, that if any negroe, molatto, Indian slave, or servant for life, runaway and shalbe persued by the warrant or hue and crye, it shall and may be lawfull for any person who shall endeavour to take them, upon the resistance of such negroe, molatto, Indian slave, or servant for life, to kill or wound him or them soe resisting;** Provided alwayes, and it is the true intent and meaning hereof, that such negroe, molatto, Indian slave, or servant for life, be named and described in the hue and crye which is alsoe to be signed by the master or owner of the said runaway. And if it happen that such negroe, molatto, Indian slave, or servant for life doe dye of any wound in such their resistance received the master or owner of such shall receive satisfaction from the publique for his negroe, molatto, Indian slave, or servant for life, soe killed or dyeing of such wounds; and the person who shall kill or wound by virtue of any such hugh and crye any such soe resisting in manner as aforesaid shall not be questioned for the same, he forthwith giveing notice thereof and returning the hue and crye or warrant to the master or owner of him or them soe killed or wounded or to the next justice of peace. And it is further enacted by the authority aforesaid that all such negroes and slaves shalbe valued at ffowre thousand five hundred pounds of tobacco and caske a peece, and Indians at three thousand pounds of tobacco and caske a peice, And further if it shall happen that any negroe, molatto, Indians slave or servant for life, in such their resistance to receive any wound whereof they may not happen to dye, but shall lye any considerable tyme sick and disabled, then alsoe the master or owner of the same soe sick or disabled shall receive from the publique a reasonable satisfaction for such damages as they shall make appeare they have susteyned thereby at the county court, who shall thereupon grant the master or owner a certificate to the next assembly of what damages they shall make appeare; And it is further enacted that the neighbouring Indians doe and hereby are required and enjoyned to seize and apprehend all runawayes whatsoever that shall happen to come amongst them, and to bring them before some justice of the peace whoe upon the receipt of such servants, slave, or slaves, from the Indians, shall pay unto the said Indians for a recompence twenty armes length of Roanoake or the value thereof in goods as the Indians shall like of, for which the said justice of peace shall receive from the publique two hundred and fifty pounds of tobacco, and the said justice to proceed in conveying the runaway to his master according to the law in such cases already provided; This act to continue in force till the next assembly and noe longer unlesse it be thought fitt to continue"

This statue defined four types of legal status for persons of color: Negro and mulatto persons, which meant those who were free or indentured; Next came "Indian slave", and finally *servant for life*. This ruling also made it legal to wound or kill a person of color who resisted arrest, and for the owner of any slave to be financially compensated. Another law – the statute of 1680 – restricted and policed the movements of slaves to meet at gatherings, including funerals. It also became illegal to physically defend oneself against unjust seizure. Then came the statute of 1691 – the first miscegenation law against interracial marriage. Other English colonies were passing similar measures and statutes. The miscegenation law also closed the loophole that the 1662 ruling did not close, that a child of color would become a slave if the mother was a slave, but the child would be free if the mother was English. Now, even if the mother was a free English woman to a child of color, her child would be bound out for thirty years. Finally, in 1705 came several more devastating enactments, including being denied the right to testify as witnesses in court, and declaring "the Negro, Mulatto, and Indian slaves within this dominion, to be real estate."

Not to say that the lives of white Indentured Servants had it any better, before slavery was finally put in place legally. There are many accounts of white Indentured servants being killed or beaten at the hands of their masters, as shown in the Virginia colony court cases. But as England entered the Slave Trade, the need for Indentured Servants dried out, and was replaced by the enslaved African. Their Virginian-born offspring were also stripped of their rights, even though they were born in a colony under the Royal Crown.

The African-descent and aboriginals of Virginia and the Carolinas would experience unimagined horrors of oppression and enslavement, especially from the 1650's to the early 1700's. Let us explore how first the indigenous were treated during this time period. The historical record speaks for itself. Here are some filed Virginia court records, also found in the reference works by Paul Heinnigg:

**Estate of Col. Moore, 26 June 1646, By two Indians sold to Wm. Berkley 0600 pds tobacco**

**By two Indians sold to John Harmon 0500 pds tobacco**

**By one Indian sold Capt. Thomas Pettus 0600**

**"Robert Jackson ... cause to be pd. Edward Adcock planter 1,200 pds tobacco 10 November next on Queen's Creek in York Parish ... as security bind one Indian mayd servant by name Mall & 3 cows."**

last day November 1646.

Surry County "I, Henerye Randolph mrcht ... sell unto Richard Attkins of Chard in the Cou[nty]_of Somersett mrcht. five cowes ... and alsoe one Indian Boy called Tom. To have and to hold the sd. Indian boy and the sd five Cowes and their increase." 17th May 1653. Record. 7 Jan. 1653/4.

Surry County 30 December 1654, Indenture Sam. Hubye of Surry planter & an Indian Boy belonginge to the people or nation of Seacocks Called in the Indian language Highamaccounte, but by the English Robert ... serve him four yeares from the day ... recorded 6 September 1655.

"I kinge of the Waineoakes doe firmely bargaine and make sale unto Elith: Short her heires a boy of my nacon named Weetoppin ... until the full terme of his life in consideration..." 2 July 1659. Recorded July 1659.

Charles City County 20 April 1663, John Busby of Surry to Mr. William Rollinson one Indian Boy about ye age of 5 years for ye term & time..."

The Indian youth lately dwelling with Mr. Rice Hoe complayning for illegal detention ... to dwell & continue with Theodorick Bland, Esq., until further claime agst. him.

3 June 1663, Petition of thomas ye Indian lately detained in service by Mr. Rice Hoe ... referred until ye next court at wch time ye said Hoe is ordered to produce & present due proof that ye said Indian was legally and justly deatined as his servt.

York County 25 June 1666, "Will an Indian Boy Servt. to Coll. Nathaniel Bacon, Esq., is adjudged to be eight years old & ordered to serve according to act."

August 1688 Robin an Indian servant to David Williamson is adjudged 7 years old.

October 1689, One Indian girle named Besse servt. to Jo: Mattux is adjudged 6 years old.

December 1689, Roger an Indian ... Richd. Bradford.

August 1690, Jenny an Indian girle belonging to Ralph Jackson 6 years old.

White settlers began moving into the Carolinas around 1650. Soon they were encroaching upon the lands and hunting grounds of the Tuscarora people. Other indigenous such as the Croatan, the Hattaras, Pee Dee, and Saponi also felt the tension (Today's Lumbee Nation are related to the Croatan and Tuscarora). But even more serious was the threat the indigenous felt of being kidnapped and sold into slavery. After the "massacre of 1644" as the historians called it, Native indigenous who were captured in warfare against the colonists were sold as slaves and transported to other colonies or to the sugar plantations in the Caribbean, such as Barbados. The kidnapping of children was a constant threat. It was so prevalent that in 1649 the Virginia Assembly passed a law against it. The law was renewed in 1658, but had no effect. When the colonists first arrived to the Indigenous lands of Virginia in 1607, it was reported that the indigenous population was 18,000. By 1676, it had dropped to 6,000. In 1700, a surveyor named John Lawson made his journey through North Carolina researching the flora and landscape of the area. He also wrote a report on his observations regarding the aboriginals who live in the region.

The settlers in South Carolina soon saw the profitability of the slave trade. The majority of slaves they dealt with during the late 1600's were captured indigenous, especially women and children, as their men were often killed in battle. South Carolina quickly learned the tactic of arming enemy tribes to attack the Tuscarora to obtain more slaves.

In 1710, an event occurred that proved to be traumatizing to the Tuscarora. A colony was established in the Albemarle area along the Neuse and Trent Rivers by Swiss and German settlers, and named it New Bern. But in so doing, the settlers encroached upon a Tuscarora village, *Chattoka*, displacing it. Tensions between the Tuscarora and different settlers had been mounting in other parts of their tribal territory. But the Tuscarora viewed the establishing of this settlement in one of their villages as too much for them to bear. They feared that more settlers would come, and more of their lands and way of life would disappear.

The tribal leaders of the Tuscarora convened to discuss their future. Should they relocate to other lands and prevent a war, which surely will break out if attacks on their people continue? In June 1710, a delegation of the Tuscarora traveled to the Provincial Government of Pennsylvania with a petition, asking for protection, and the desire to relocate to Pennsylvania lands. The Tuscarora met with representatives sent by the Provincial Governor on June 8, 1810 at Conestoga, and presented eight wampum belts – each belt symbolizing each of the tribe's grievances and wishes. The tribal chiefs from the Five Nations Iroquois were also present. A report of the meeting was made by the Pennsylvania commissioners who were present, which today is preserved at the Pennsylvania State Archives.

Here is what the Tuscarora presented:

At Conestogo, June 8th, 1710.

Present:

John French.

Henry Worley.

Iwaagenst Terrutawanaren, & Teonnottein, Chiefs of the Tuscaroroes, Civility, the Seneques Kings, & four Chief more of yt nacon, wth. Opessa y<sup>e</sup> Shawanois King.

The Indians were told that acording to their Request we were come from the Govr. & Govmt., to hear what proposals they had to make anent a peace, according to the purport of their Embassy from their own People.

They signified to us by a Belt of Wampum, which was sent from their old Woman, that those Implored their friendship of the Christians & Indians of this Govmt., that without danger or trouble they might fetch wood & Water.

The second Belt was sent from their children born, & those yet in the womb, Requesting that Room to sport & Play **without danger of Slavery**, might be allowed them.

The third Belt was sent from their young men fitt to Hunt, that privilege to leave their Towns, & seek Provision for their aged, might be granted to them **without fear of Death or Slavery.**

The fourth was sent from the men of age, Requesting that the Wood, by a happy peace, might be as safe for them as their forts.

The fifth was sent from the whole nation, requesting peace, that thereby they might have Liberty to visit their Neighbours.

The sixth was sent from their Kings & Chiefs, Desiring a lasting peace with the Christians and Indians of this Govmt., that thereby they might be secured against those fearful apprehensions they have these several years felt.

The seventh was sent in order to intreat a Cessation from murdering & taking them, that by the allowance thereof, they may not be affraid of a mouse, or any other thing that Ruffles the Leaves.

The Eight was sent to declare, that as being hitherto Strangers to this Place, they now Came as People blind, no path nor Communicacon being betwixt us & them; but now they hope we will take them by the hand & lead them, & then they will lift up their heads in the woods without danger or fear.

These Belts (they say) are only sent as an Introduction, & in order to break off hostilities till next Spring, for then their Kings will Come & sue for the peace they so much Desire.

We acquainted them that as most of this Continent were the subjects of the Crown of Great Britain, tho' divided into several Govmts.; So it is expected their Intentions are not only peaceable towards us, but also to all the subjects of the Crown; & that if they intend to settle & live amicably here, they need not Doubt the protection of this Govmt. in such things as were honest & good, but that to Confirm the sincerity of their past Carriage towards the English, & to raise in us a good opinion of them, it would be very necessary to procure a Certificate from the Govmt. they leave, to this, of their Good behaviour, & then they might be assured of a favourable reception.

The Seneques return their hearty thanks to the Govmt. for their Trouble in sending to them, And acquainted us that by advice of a Council amongst them it was Determined to send these belts, brought by the Tuscaroroes, to the five nations.

May it please your honr.

Pursuant to your honrs. & Council's Orders, we went to Conestogo, where the forewritten Contents were by the Chiefs of the Tuscaroroes to us Deliver'd; the sincerity of their Intentions we Cannot anywise Doubt, since they are of the same race & Language with our Seneques, who have always proved trusty, & have also for these many years been neighbors to a Govmt. Jealous of Indians, And yet not Displeased with them; wishing your honr. all happiness, we remain,

Your honrs. Most humble & Obliged servants,

**JOHN FFRENCH**,

**HENRY WORLEY**.

The commissioners of the provincial council, however, did not grant the Tuscarora permission to relocate. Instead, they proposed:

"that to Confirm the sincerity of their past Carriage towards the English, & to raise in us a good opinion of them, it would be very necessary to procure a Certificate from the Govmt. they leave, to this, of their Good behaviour, & then they might be assured of a favourable reception"

The tribal delegation returned to North Carolina, their effort to avoid war by moving to a peaceful land having failed. What would they do now?

At this time, it was reported the Tuscarora in North Carolina were made up of two primary groups, a northern branch headed by Chief Tom Blunt in the present-day area of Bertie County, and a southern branch headed by Chief Hancock in the area of New Bern. The territory headed by Chief Hancock was the area where their village *Chattoka* had been replaced with the Swiss colony's new town, New Bern.

In early September, the Tuscarora capture surveyor John Lawson and Baron von Graffenried, the founder of the colony New Bern, along with two enslaved persons whose names are unknown. Lawson is killed during the incident, but the Tuscarora spare the two enslaved persons and von Graffenried. On September 22, 1711, the Tuscarora and other allied tribes made a surprise attack on the settlers in Bath County. More than 130 colonists were killed. The North Carolina Governor called out the militia and also sent for help from South Carolina. Besides the Tuscarora who were killed, at least 700 of them were taken prisoner and sold into slavery, including women and children. After the defeat, the Tuscarora split into three directions. Many went to New York to join the Iroquois Confederacy. Others fled to Virginia, while several remained in North Carolina and later settled on a reservation in the area of Bertie County along the Roanoke River. Eventually over time, many of the families left the reservation and assimilated into North Carolina's general population. By 1755, there was a population of about 300 indigenous living on the reservation, called "Indian Woods." By 1804, it was reported that only 10 to 20 families remained at the reservation. Later, a number of indigenous were found to be living in Robeson County.

Are there descendants of the Tuscarora who are still living? Yes. Likewise, could there be descendants today from the vast number of Tuscarora people who were sold away as slaves? One African American family from Cross County, Arkansas have an interesting oral story in their family that was passed down. Their ancestors, Caroline Binford, Peggy Campbell Binford, and Clara Campbell – who had moved to Cross County by early as 1885 – had moved from a plantation in Montgomery County, Mississippi where they had once lived as enslaved people. The ancestors, who were all born in North Carolina between 1800 – 1828, said they had descended from a Native woman whose name was Betsie Hunt. They also said Betsie had never been enslaved, and she was either Cherokee or Tuscarora. Could their oral account be documented and proven true?

Records show that the women Caroline, Peggy, and Clara were listed on the 1870 Federal Census of Carroll County, Mississippi – the county's name at the time, before part of the county later became Montgomery County by 1880. Research shows that three former slave owners lived nearby the women – John Ambrose Binford, Benjamin Campbell, and his son Charles C.P. Campbell – all from Halifax County, North Carolina. By 1840, they had left North Carolina with their slaves and moved to Carroll County, Mississippi. Records reveal that another planter – Henry H. Burt of Halifax County – also moved to Carroll County by 1840. On March 4, 1841, Henry H. Burt sold Charles C.P. Campbell a land deed and twenty-one enslaved, which included nine females – Clary, Violet, Carolina, Patty, Lizzy, Jiney, Charlot, Mariah, and Ferely. Research was inconclusive, however, as to whether the female names Clary and Carolina, listed in the deed, were two of the actual ancestors of the family from Cross County, Arkansas. Nonetheless, the women Caroline, Peggy, and Clara, all three reported in 1870 – as recorded on the census – that they were born in North Carolina. So now, what about Betsie Hunt? Could documentation on this part of the oral family story be found?

Records show there was a woman named "Betsey Hunt" listed on the 1850 Federal Census for North Carolina, at the age of eighty and born around 1770. She was enumerated with a mulatto family by the name of Oxendine in Robeson County, which happened to be the same county where it was reported many indigenous families had migrated, including descendants of the Tuscarora and Croatan. Another "mulatto" family listed five houses away from Betsey Hunt and the Oxendines in Robeson County was also noted. It was a family by the name of Chavis. In the federal census records, not only was the term "Mulatto" referring to persons who were of African descent, but the racial classification also at times referred to indigenous persons. The name "Betsey Hunt" also showed up listed in subsequent federal censuses and death records for Robeson County, including a Betsy Oxendine Hunt, the wife of Jesse Hunt who was born about 1830, and ancestry listed as "Indian." The Chavis families of Robeson County were also listed as "Indian", and intermarried with families named Sweat, Lowery, Kearsey, Berry, and others.

DNA testing today is connecting many persons to their indigenous ancestry, including those found in Robeson County, North Carolina, many of whom identify with Lumbee. During World War II, many Lumbee began migrating to Baltimore, Maryland. According to colonial court records, many American families began as African, indigenous, and European intermarriages in colonial America. With DNA testing being a new tool for genealogists, it is fascinating as well as mind-boggling to explore how your own unique family came about. Rather than identifying oneself as either "this race or that," many today are identifying as dual, tri-racial, or more ethnic lines. *Do you embrace and acknowledge ALL of your DNA ancestry?* In conclusion, the oral story that was passed down in the family of Cross County, Arkansas about Betsie Hunt, a Tuscarora woman whose children had been sold into slavery and taken to Mississippi, has a very, very strong ring of truth. Other persons today who are searching their indigenous roots have similar stories.

Here are a few Runaway Slave newspaper notices, and Court records pertaining to the indigenous of North Carolina and Virginia:

**Lancaster County, VA**

**September 1710, Ned an Indian a Runaway Slave belonging to William Dawes of North Carolina.**

**2 August 1770** (Rind edition). Committed to the prison of York, a Negro boy, who says that he is free and was born in the Indian town on Pamunkey river.

**12 September 1771.** Prince George. Run away from the subscriber a Negro fellow named Frank, twenty seven years of age, five feet five or six inches high, of a yellow Complexion ... He has run away several times and always passed for a Freeman ... I imagine he is sculking about Indian Town on Pamunkey among the Indians, as in one of his former Trips he got himself a Wife amongst them. David Scott.

**12 March 1772.** Run away from the subscriber in Dinwiddie ... Mulatto man named Dick, about 30 years old ... has grey eyes, his hair is short, and curls close to his head ... a Shoemaker by Trade and is very handy about any other business; he may try to pass for a free man, as he can read and write ... has got a brother belonging to Mr. David Scott, of

Prince George, who has been run away for a year or two together, and brought several times from among the Indians on Pamunkey river, they will probably make that way together ... James Walker.

**26 November 1772.** (Purdie & Dixon) Run away from the subscriber in Cumberland a Mulatto Man named Jim who is a slave but pretends to have a right to his freedom. His Father was an Indian, of the name of Cheshire, and very likely will call himself James Cheshire, or Chink. He is a short well set fellow, about twenty seven years of age, with long black hair resembling an Indian's. Paul Michaux.

**10 March 1774.** (Rind edition) Run away from the subscriber a half Indian fellow who calls himself Jack Brown, and was formerly the property of Colonel John Bolling, of Goochland; he is about 40 years old. Augustine Longan.

**2 December 1775. Bute County, North Carolina.** Run away from William Tabb, a Slave named Charles, of the Indian Breed, about 23 Years of Age, with straight black Hair, light Complexion ... raised in Prince George County, Virginia ... William Tabb. Robert Goodloe.

**Augusta County, VA**

**p. 206, 19 August 1777, Nat an Indian boy in the custody of Mary Greenlee who detains him as a slave complains that he is held in unlawful slavery. Commission to take depositions in Carolina or else where.**

p.230, 17 September 1777, On the complaint of Nat an Indian or Mustee Boy who says he is detained by Mary Greenlee...

p. 308, Petition of Nat a Mullatoe or Indian Boy to be set free from service of Mary Greenlee...nothing appeared to the Court but a bill of sale for Ten Pounds from one Sherwood Harris of Granville County, North Carolina that through several assignments was made over to James Greenlee deceased, late husband to the said Mary...said Mullatoe or Indian Boy is a free man & no slave.

There is evidence also that enslaved persons in Virginia had come even from the regions of East India:

### Spotsylvania County

p.440, Zachary Lewis, Churchwarden of St. George Parish, presents Ann Jones, a servant belonging to John West, who declared that Pompey an East Indian (slave) belonging to William Woodford, Gent., was the father of sd child which was adjudged of by the Court that she was not under the law having a Mullato child, that only relates to Negroes and Mullatoes and being Silent as to Indians, carry sd. Ann Jones to the whipping post.

### Richmond County

p.111, 6 February 1705/6, Petition of Sembo, an East India Indian Servant to Jno. Lloyd, Esq., for his freedom.

p.156-9, Petition of Moota, an East India Indian, servant to Capt. Thomas Beale, surviving executor of Mr. William Colston, deced., for his freedom ... ordered and judged that said Moota be free ... ordered and adjudged that said Sembo be free.

"Broke out of Prince George's County jail, on the 21st of May at Night, one Thomas Mayhew, of a very dark Complexion, (his Father being an East-India Indian) about 5 feet 9 inches high, wears his own Hair which is very Black. He formerly lived in the lower end of that County. Whoever takes up the said Mayhew, and brings him to Upper-Marlborough, to the Subscriber, shall receive Two Pistoles Reward."

Benjamin Brookes

Slavery would continue to spread and deepen within the Southern States, including Virginia and North Carolina, affecting persons of African and indigenous descent for generations. Families would continue to be separated and broken apart, oftentimes never to see each other again, as they were sold into slavery. Slave owners would "bequeath" enslaved family members to their own family in their last wills and testaments, as the slave owner's wife, children, and grandchildren would "inherit" a "slave for life." And if that enslaved person produced children, then those children would be "bequeathed" to the next slave-owning generation. One example of this is the enslaved persons who were owned by Samuel Eskridge of Westmoreland County, Virginia at the time of his death in 1747:

Estate of Samuel Eskridge gentleman Deceased
Joseph Clark

William Clark

Benjamin Clark

Elizabeth Clark

Will

George

Tom

Hannah

Jenny

Akey

**Recorded the 20ᵗʰ day of October 1747**

Samuel Eskridge (son of Colonel George Eskridge of Sandy Point), at the time of his death had three minor age sons, Richard, Burdett, and John. The Probate Court proceeded to break up the enslaved family and award them to Eskridge's sons:

WESTMORELAND COUNTY, VIRGINIA
ORPHAN DISTRIBUTIONS
SAMUEL ESKRIDGE, DECD

"The Negroes belonging to the said Richard Eskridge as given by the said allotment are **WILLIAM CLARK a Negro man, TOM, a Negro boy, and HANNAH a Negro woman;**

"The Negroes belonging to the said Burdett Eskridge as given by the said allotment are **GEORGE** a Negro man, BESS a Negro woman, and **JENNY** a Negro girl, Witness our hands this 30ᵗʰ day of November 1756

"The Negroes belonging to the said John Eskridge as given by the said allotment are **BENJ CLARK** a Negro man, NAN a Negro woman and BECK her child…the said Beck is now dead"

Witness our hands this 30th day of November 1756

The son Burdett later married and migrated to South Carolina, taking George, Bess, and the girl Jenny with him (see the book *Akee Tree*, by the author, 2013 edition). The son John remained in Virginia, while the third son Richard removed to Caswell County, North Carolina, taking with him William Clark, Tom, and Hannah. Records show that Tom was still alive when Richard Eskridge died in 1816:

BOOK G CASWELL COUNTY, NORTH CAROLINA

PAGE 124 RICHARD ESKRIDGE

'I give and bequeath to my well beloved wife Elizabeth Eskridge **my old Negro man Slave TOM,** one Negro woman named Rachel, & her youngest child Anne.

The above mentioned property to be hers forever to be disposed of by her in any manner she may think proper among her children; Also my will & desire is that she continue to possess & enjoy the whole of my other Negroes during her lifetime…& further if there should be any increase among my Negroes after the date of this will the said increase shall be hers….after my wife's death, I give and bequeath to my son Thomas Eskridge one Negro man Slave by the name of BEN

I also give & bequeath unto my son Burdit Eskridge one Negro boy by the name of ADAM;

I give and bequeath unto my son John Eskridge two Negro girls, one named ALHA and the other HESWILLY

I give and bequeath unto my son William Eskridge two young Negroes named SIMON and HALE, likewise my shot gun &

———————

To my daughter Rebecca one Negro woman by the name of ANNE

To my daughter Anne one Negro Girl by the name of HENRIETTA which she hath already in possession

To my daughter Martha two Negro Girls, one by the name of LUCY & the other MOLL...."

Signed , Sealed & Acknowledged

In the presence of

Gabe Lea
&
Vincent Lea                          State of North Carolina
                                     Caswell County

January Court 1816"

The enslaved man Tom no doubt would have kept the memory of his separated family and hold on dearly to the first names of his kin, such as Hannah, George, and others. The will in 1816 mentioned "my *other* Negroes...& further if there should be any *increase* among my Negroes..." indicating other un-named persons were on the plantation, as well as possible children born in the future. Name patterns in genealogy are very important clues, especially when constructing family genealogies from slavery. This has proven true regarding the Eskridge family, as we shall see regarding two enslaved women, Hannah and Phillis.

Richard Eskridge of Caswell County, North Carolina had several children, some moving to Nashville and Winchester, Tennessee, and Mississippi (See Sources, Chapter Nine, under Eskridge). Others of the Eskridge family from Virginia went to Ohio and Kentucky, such as *Kentucky George*, a revolutionary war soldier who settled in Grayson County, Kentucky with nine enslaved persons. One of Richard's sons, also named Richard, died in Rutherford County, North Carolina. His last will, dated November 3, 1831 reads:

"I give unto my beloved wife Elizabeth my Negro woman **Hannah** to dispose of as she pleases, & her increase also forever…I give unto my wife all the following Negroes to wit, Negro man Ivin, Negro woman **Phillis**, and all her children…"

Records between 1867 and 1880 show two women of African descent, Hannah Eskridge, born in 1776, and Phyllis Eskridge, born in 1820, were living in the town of Duck Hill, Mississippi. Freedmen Bureau records show that Phyllis and her husband, George Eskridge, appealed to the Freedmen Bureau for help to safely transport their daughter from *Raleigh, North Carolina* to Duck Hill:

*North Carolina Freedmen's Bureau*

*1867*

*July 2 Received. Approved if circumstances are as stated.*

*Eskridge Geo & Phyllis Duck Hill, Miss June 10 67*

*"Request that their daughter Eileen now in Raleigh, be given transportation to Miss."*

Details as to the reason for George and Phyllis' request is unknown, however, the atmosphere of unrest in the southern States during that time in history – Reconstruction – provides a context. A violent Civil war had just recently ended, and three hundred years of slavery codes, which controlled the lives of people of color, had finally been destroyed in the flames. An old order had passed away, never to come back. People of African descent and others of color had entered a new era in determining their legal free status, a status not had since the early 1660's in Colonial Virginia prior to the first slave laws. But along with the destruction of the old system came hatred and fear from those who regarded the old way as a devastating loss. As a result, people of African descent and those of color in the former Confederate States faced all kinds of attacks, even threats of death. North Carolina after the Civil War was no exception. In Raleigh, freedmen poured into the city after the war seeking assistance and jobs. Hostility from whites in the city was high. There were also many reports of physical violence and attempted assaults by Whites against Blacks and by Blacks against Whites. In 1867, the Freedmen's Bureau in charge of North Carolina were flooded with reports and complaints every month involving assault, battery, use of a deadly weapon, rape, and attempted rape. On June 6, 1867 a hanging was reported. Under this climate, George and Phyllis Eskridge asked for soldier escort of their daughter to reach Mississippi.

So far, no record has yet to turn up explaining what happened to daughter Eileen. George and Phyllis had other children – Frank, Louis, William Harrison, Doc, and very likely two others named Booker and Mitch – all living in Duck Hill and raising families. By

1880, Phyllis had been a widow for at least ten years, and Hannah had turned 104. Hannah Eskridge was likely the grandmother of Phyllis. Both of their names link back to the enslaved North Carolina family in 1831. Finally, records reveal that Hannah, Phyllis, and their families were living on land plots given to them after the Civil War. The plots were once part of a particular slave owner's land. His name was also Richard Eskridge, a planter in Edgefield, South Carolina who operated a plantation with his brother Samuel Eskridge in Tennessee, then migrated to Alabama with his other brother Austin Pollard Eskridge, before finally settling in Duck Hill, Mississippi by 1834 (See Sources, Chapter Nine, under Eskridge). Amazingly, DNA testing is connecting the living descendants of that separated family today. The historic events of the year 2020 is also generating a connection and dialogue among Black and White descendants of those who share the Eskridge surname in the United States. Stories such as these are being shared from other families who are doing similarly – talking about race – and many for the first time.

So as discussed, the events in Virginia from 1619 and in New York from 1626 – laid the groundwork for legalized slavery in the United States. What forms of oppression does history reveal in other parts of the world? What seems to be a recurring theme in this book about man's history? And what does this recurring theme reveal about mankind's future?

# CHAPTER TEN

# Religion's Involvement in the Slave Trade

ROMAN EMPEROR THEODOSIUS I DIED on January 17, 395 CE. Thus, the Roman Empire was divided between his two sons – Honorius and Arcadius. Arcadius received the eastern part of the empire, which included Syria, Egypt, and Constantinople, which had become the new capital of the empire when Emperor Constantine had earlier moved the capital from Rome. The Eastern Roman Empire would eventually end on May 29, 1453, when Sultan Mehmed II overthrew Constantinople.

The other son, Honorius, received the western part of the Roman Empire, which included North Africa, Italy, Spain, Gaul, Germania, and Britannia. Even before Honorius received his legal portion, Germanic tribes, such as the Franks and Saxons, were invading Roman territory and settling in an area in present-day Germany.

On December 25, 800 CE, Pope Leo III chose the Frank, King Charles, as Emperor of the Holy Roman Empire, crowning him on the annual Roman Festival of *Saturnalia* – pagan rites in the worship of the Sun – celebrated on December 25 (now called Christmas). Emperor King Charles was later referred to by another name, Charlemagne. Pope Leo III, and all other popes after him for the next one thousand years – as well as the Roman Catholic Church –

would now consider the Holy Roman Emperor – the Caesar or *Kaiser* – the legal successor of the Roman Empire. In fact, over time, the title "Holy Roman Emperor" would later be viewed in conjunction with the title "King of Germany."

However, prior to the crowning of a Holy Roman Emperor by the Catholic pope, other major events in world affairs had taken place nearly two hundred years earlier. In 632 CE, the prophet Muhammad died. In 638, the city of Jerusalem came under the domain of Umar ibn al-Khattab, the Caliph of the Rashidun Caliphate. Umar was the successor of Caliph Abu Bakr, who had succeeded Muhammad. But after Umar's assassination in 644, other caliphs followed. By 692 CE, an Islamic shrine was built on the site of the Jewish temple that had been destroyed by the Roman armies in 70 CE. This Islamic shrine was called the Dome of the Rock.

Beginning in the late 11th Century, the city of Jerusalem would become embroiled in several battles for its control. In 1071 CE, the Muslim Seljuk Turks ripped Jerusalem away from the Fatimid Caliphate dynasty. By 1095 CE, Pope Urban II proclaimed a war against the Turks and all other Muslims. Called the *Crusades*, these wars became a series of military campaigns organized by the Catholic Church to take Jerusalem from Muslim control. Then, in 1098, The Fatimid Caliphate recaptured Jerusalem. This was followed by a war with the Crusaders taking Jerusalem in 1099. There would be seven more such "Crusades" between 1099 – 1270 CE. These religious wars never did bring true peace and unity to the descendants of Shem, Ham, and Japheth. Instead, the Catholic Church's doctrine of *Imperial Immediacy* was born, under which the *Imperial Estates* of the Holy Roman Empire, such as Imperial cities, prince-Bishoprics, secular principalities, and Individuals, such as the Imperial Knights, *were declared free from the authority of any local Lord*, and placed under the direct authority of the so-called Holy Roman Emperor. And as previously discussed (Chapter Seven), the church's sanction of the Atlantic Slave Trade to the Americas led to the acquisition of more Imperial Estates. On 18 June 1452, Pope Nicholas V issued a Papal Bull entitled *Dum Diversas* – granting Portugal the "right" to subdue all "pagans" to "perpetual servitude." Pope Nicholas V issued another Papal Bull on 8 January 1455, *Romanus Pontifex*, reaffirming his earlier grant to Portugal, and specifically addressing the King of the Portuguese Crown, Afonso V (Alphonso V) with these words:

"We weighing all and singular the premises with due meditation, and noting that since we had formerly by other letters of ours granted among other things free and ample faculty to the aforesaid King Alfonso – to invade, search out, capture, vanquish, and subdue all Saracens and pagans whatsoever, and other enemies of Christ wheresoever placed, and the kingdoms, dukedoms, principalities, dominions, possessions, and all movable and immovable goods whatsoever held and possessed by them and to reduce their persons to perpetual slavery, and to apply and appropriate to himself and his successors the kingdoms, dukedoms, counties, principalities, dominions, possessions, and goods, and to convert them to his and their use and profit…"

And, as also noted previously, Pope Alexander VI issued two Papal Bulls on 3 May 1493, granting the Monarchy of Spain the same permissions and favors as Portugal to poach and raid West and Central Africa – and subdue humans they chose to perpetual slavery.

Eight years later – on 16 September 1501 – King Ferdinand II and Queen Isabella of Spain sent a letter to the governor of Spanish Haiti:

"Because with great care we have procured the conversion of the Indians to our Holy Catholic Faith, and furthermore, if there are still people there who are doubtful of the faith in their own conversions, it would be a hindrance, and therefore we will not permit, nor allow to go there Moors, nor Jews nor heretics nor reconciled heretics, nor persons who are recently converted to our faith, except if they are black slaves, or other slaves, that have been born under the dominion of our natural Christian subjects."

Besides Christendom, it should also be pointed out that African and Arab religious influence also played a part in the sanctioning of the international slave trade. All of this reminds one of the words in the book called *Apokalupsis* in Greek, taken from a vision by the last living Apostle of Jesus, at the age of ninety-nine. Notice how the apostle named John described the complicity of religious involvement in the slave trade:

> *"One of the seven angels who had the seven bowls came and said to me: Come, I will show you the judgement on the great prostitute who sits on many waters…**Babylon the Great**…a full cargo of gold, silver, precious stones, pearls…cattle, sheep, horses, carriages, **slaves, and human beings.**"*

In 1516, Pope Leo X bestowed his papal coronation upon Charles V as the new Holy Roman Emperor and monarch of Spain, and Archduke of Austria. Two years after his coronation, Charles V granted a charter on 18 August 1518 for permission to transport 4,000 enslaved people directly from the continent of Africa to Haiti, Cuba, and Puerto Rico. The Imperial Estates of Spanish Mexico and Spanish Florida were later added. But what about France? Did she share responsibility and become complicit in the enslaving of her own cousins too?

In 1682, the French explorer Robert Cavelier de La Salle named an area in the Americas *Louisiana*, after the French king Louis XIV. The Louisiana Territory at that time stretched from parts of Canada and present-day Montana, Wyoming, Colorado, New Mexico, North & South Dakota, Minnesota, Iowa, Nebraska, Missouri, Kansas, Oklahoma, Arkansas, and New Orleans Territory. Numerous Indigenous tribes dotted the Louisiana region, such as the Blackfeet, Lakota Sioux, the Ottawa Potawatomi, the Miami Illinois, the Fox Sauk Kickapoo, the Biloxi, the Choctaw & Chickasaw, the Creek, Natchez, Quapaw, and the Chitimacha, to name a few. The French began enslaving the Indigenous in the Lower Mississippi Valley. By the time of the 1708 Louisiana Census, the French had listed eighty enslaved Indigenous, listed as "savages." French soldiers engaged in slave raids. French Canadian soldiers, for example, raided the entire Chitimacha village on Bayou Lafourche, and sold the women and children into slavery. In 1762, France ceded Louisiana to Spain, and then after thirty-eight years of Spanish rule the Spanish ceded Louisiana back to France in 1802.

Saint Domingue was a French colony in Haiti around 1660. In 1697, the French acquired the island of Haiti from Spain. They renamed the island Saint Domingue, and began importing Africans for their use, fusing them together with enslaved Africans already brought to the island from the Spanish. Saint Domingue had become France's wealthiest colony, due to the production of sugar, off the backs of enslaved Indigenous and African labor. A revolution in Haiti began in 1791, when the enslaved Africans rose up against their masters. The Haitian revolution, which preceded the French Revolution, went on for several years and led by several leaders, including a free man of color named Toussaint Louverture, who, historians say, received education from his godfather Pierre Baptiste, a free person of color who lived on the Breda plantation. Toussaint, on August 29,

1793, declared liberty and equality to all persons of color on Haiti. Louverture, and the generals who sided with him, at first proposed reforms in the French colony rather than a complete destruction of the French colonial government. In 1797, Louverture was promoted to Governor General of Saint Domigue.

In France, Napoleon Bonaparte gained power in 1799. When hearing abut the situation in Haiti, Napoleon acknowledged Louverture's position and promised to uphold the abolition of slavery in the island colony. But Napoleon feared that Louverture would carry the revolution into neighboring Spanish Santo Domingo (Dominican Republic). When Louverture invaded Santo Domingo in January 1801 and then later presented a new Constitution on July 7, Napoleon sent 20,000 French soldiers in an attempt to restore French rule and to arrest all Black officials for deportation. Toussaint Louverture was arrested and deported to France in July 1802, where he died in prison in 1803, the same year Napoleon ceded Louisiana to the United States. Napoleon's soldiers in Haiti, however, were eventually weakened by yellow fever on the island, as the revolutionary soldiers under Toussaint and his generals remained hidden while the yellow fever season raged. In 1804, Napoleon's soldiers in Haiti were defeated and evacuated the island, leading to Haiti's Independence.

Two years later, in the year 1806, was the fall of the so-called Holy Roman Empire. This was a result of Napoleon's election which gave him the title *Emperor of the French*, at the same time Francis II was sitting as the Holy Roman Emperor. To upstage Napoleon, Francis II created another title and declared himself also the *Emperor of Austria*, which was part of the German Confederation. But Napoleon was not yet finished. In 1806, he created the *Confederation of the Rhine* and Napoleon as *Protector*. He also called upon Francis II to abdicate his throne. There was fear among those in the papal hierarchy that Napoleon might even go so far as to proclaim himself the Holy Roman Emperor. To prevent that possibility, Francis II not only abdicated from his throne, but also dissolved the Holy Roman Empire, replacing it for the Austrian (German) Empire that Francis II had created. Thus, the western part of the Holy Roman Empire came to its end in 1806 by this way. Yet, what happened to the Papacy? What occurred in 1870?

On September 20, 1870, the Kingdom of Italy entered Rome and overthrew the Pope, keeping him prisoner in the Vatican City for the next fifty-nine years. Those who opposed the Italian kingship in favor of supporting the Pope were the black nobility or black aristocracy, members and descendants of powerful families, Counts, Knights, Dames, Dukes, Princes, who for centuries had a connection to the Vatican. Nobility titles of these families and individuals were granted by popes. They also assisted in the governing of the Church's Imperial estates – Catholic countries. The right to membership in this Imperial aristocracy was transmitted not only to a noble's sons and grandsons but also to the groom of his daughter. Many of these families are still in existence. Likewise, self-identity to the German, Austrian, and Spanish nobility that survived the fall of the Holy Roman Empire still remain strong in the 21st century. For example, the grandchildren of Francis II – the last person who held the title Holy Roman Emperor – were Maximillan of Mexico; Maria II of Portugal; Pedro II of Brazil; Franz Joseph I of Austria. There are also descendants today of monarchs in Asia and Africa as well.

On November 15, 1884, representatives from 12 European countries and the United States began meeting in Berlin, Germany for a conference to discuss trade regulations and colonization of Africa. The discussion, which ended on February 26, 1885, was called the Berlin Conference, calling for renewed and coordinated efforts of

European interests in Africa, resulting in further exploitation of the African peoples and the elimination of African monarchies and self-governing territories. The Berlin Conference was unofficially referred to as *The Scramble for Africa*. Besides Germany and the United States, the other countries represented at the conference were: Austria-Hungary, Belgium, Denmark, Sweden-Norway, Italy, Portugal, the Ottoman Empire, Russia, and four other empires who were instrumental in the Atlantic Slave Trade. Out of those four empires, one of them rose to world dominance over the others. Who were they?

In every culture, tribe, or tongue, there have always been the medicine men, the soothsayers, the prophets – who spoke out and prophesized for the preservation and protection of their people. Whether Confucius, Nostradamis, Lone Man, or Elisha – people looked to them for signs and portents, to help lead a nation to its destination. Most often, many proved to be false prophets, as they sanctioned oppression to their fellow man. What is the theme of this book? From the beginning, we have visited the ancient empires of Africa – Assyria – Babylon – Medo-Persia – Greece – Rome. All of those nations were related to each other. But as the chronology of time went by, the descendants of the nations continued becoming far distant and separated from each other.

An ancient saying of Taoism: "Oversharpen the blade, and the edge will soon blunt; Amass a store of gold and jade, and no one can protect it; Claim wealth and titles, and disaster will follow." In regard to four empires who would enrich themselves, notice what the prophet Daniel, the dream reader, uttered about one of them in book 22 of the *Hagiographa*:

> *"Four great beasts came up from the sea, diverse one from another...*
> *and behold, there came up among them another little horn, before*

*whom there were three of the first horns plucked up by the roots: and, behold, in this horn were eyes like the eyes of man, and a mouth speaking great things...and he will humiliate three kings."*

Three horns against a little horn, and yet the little horn proved greater. Who could fit the description in our modern day? The Spanish, the Dutch, the French – all of them were masters of the Sea, possessing ships and naval fleets for the purpose of enslaving their fellow human, via the Middle Passage. But the Royal Navy of Britain proved their maritime supremacy against those three empires and became the world's most powerful navy, and the greatest empire baron of land acquisition. For example, between 1795 – 1803, Britain decided to become the aggressor and occupy Cape Town, rather than allow Napoleon. At the end of the Napoleon wars, South Africa was ceded to Britain. Diamonds were discovered in South Africa in 1867. Britain, as well as the South African Republic (founded by Dutch settlers and known as *Voortrekkers* or Boers, who would later in 1948 establish the Afrikaner National Party and classify all people into three races calling it Apartheid) declared wars on the African indigenous in order to gain control of the economic resources found in the lands. In 1879, the king of the *Bapedi*, Sekhukhune I, son of Sekwati I, son of Thulare, was defeated, captured, and imprisoned in Pretoria. Another kingdom also tried to protect the rights of their lands. Who were they?

The founder of the Zulu clan was Zula I kaMalandela (1627 – 1709), son of Malandela. A long line of king chiefs after him followed, including King Shaka (Shaka KaSenzangakhona) who ruled from 1816 – 1828. During the formation of his kingdom the *Mfecne* (crushing, scattering) occurred, a time of widespread unrest among the indigenous peoples living between the Tugela and Pongola rivers. Gold was found in 1884. By 1887, Britain maneuvered with her political laws of mediatisation, and annexed Zululand, no longer recognizing the legitimacy of any present or future Zulu chiefdom.

Britain later partnered with the United States during World War I. The result was a dual world power, a mutual protectorate alliance for their common interests. By December 1914, the United Kingdom and the Vatican re-established relations, after relations had been broken since 1570. The United States, with moral support from the Protestant churches, allied with the United Kingdom and entered the war, sending young Americans to their deaths. Religion's guilt in assisting national and state oppression continues even today. The reaping of profits to institutions, corporations, and business agents, instead of reparation equity, were sown during the complicity in the slave trade.

At the end of World War I, Britain acquired Palestine, home to Palestinian Arabs, and assigned it a Mandate until May 1948. The United Nations adopted a resolution that would divide the mandate into Jewish and Arab States when the British mandate ran out in May 1948, resulting in an Israeli State. It also created a displacement of people that has yet to be resolved. History has shown the deadly mixture of Religion and State. In 66 CE, there was an insurrection against the Roman Government by Jewish zealots – terrorists – who seized a Roman garrison full of weapons, similar to Harper's Ferry. The terrorists fought the Romans four years. Then in 70 CE, the Roman armies under General Titus marched toward Jerusalem, destroying the Jewish temple and placing the city under siege. Over a million died. It was a *Great Tribulation*. But the Roman Empire finally fell. Britannia, once a tribe in the Roman Empire, eventually rose to power. Perhaps it is so, that the prophet's dream about a little horn later rising to power had fulfillment. But – one should be reminded – Daniel had another dream, predicting that a *greater tribulation* would occur again. When?

Hausa Women in Nigeria, 2007.

Palestinian Women in Ramallah, West Bank.

Jerusalem market.

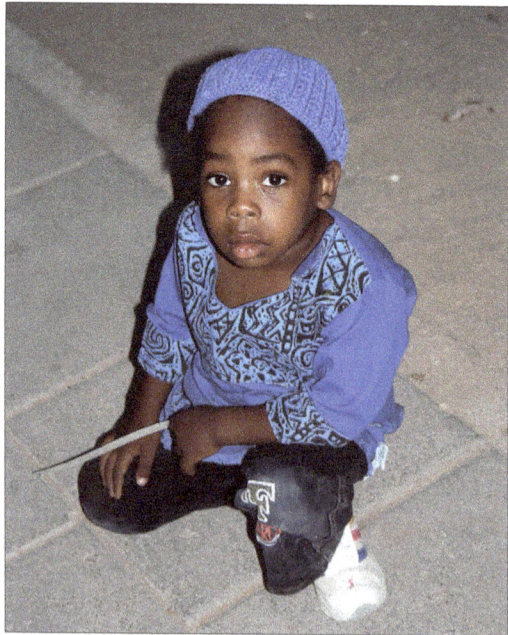

Jewish Child in
Dimona, Israel.

Free Woman of Color with daughter in New Orleans, Late 18th century collage painting, artist unknown.

Free Women of Color with their children and servants in a landscape (in Dominica), by Agostino Brunias, between 1764 – 1796.

CHAPTER ELEVEN

# The World's Ancestry – Our Future?

CHIEF JOSEPH OF THE NEZ Perce once said: "I am tired of talk that comes to nothing. It makes my heart sick when I remember all the good words and all the broken promises." Abraham Lincoln said this: "The enslaving of any race of men, or any man, and that those who did so braved the arm of Jehovah – that when a nation thus dared the Almighty every friend of that nation had cause to dread His wrath."

The sentiment of those two quotes sum up perfectly the theme of this book. War, Power, and Oppression. Those three things sadly, have plagued the ancestry of the world since man's inception. This is not to say that the human family has not shown care and compassion for one another regardless of culture, language, or appearance. There is something inherently embedded in each person the potential to display kindness and empathy. But that does not mean that everyone will. We all know way to well that a person's inborn desire for kindness can be suppressed. People can be taught hate and biases from an early age, depending on their environment. The human family, for some reason, have not been able to phase out war, power, and oppression. Not yet, to be fair. But how much more time will it take until we do? Another way of saying it is, does the human family have *enough time left* to figure it out? The serious issues now facing mankind – racism, global warming, poverty, homelessness, pandemics, exploitation of earth's resources, brutality, wars, insurrections. The list goes on. Is mankind facing extinction if these challenges continue to worsen?

When Abraham Lincoln uttered his words at the beginning of this chapter, it was a speech he gave in Columbus, Ohio in September 1859 – fourteen months before he was elected as the Sixteenth President of the United States. The climate in the country at that time, in favor of free legal status for all People of Color, was nonexistent, unless one was a person of color or an abolitionist. Three years earlier in 1856, the president-elect at the time – President James Buchanan – had made a comment on his inauguration day about the Supreme Court case of Dred Scott before the court had yet made its ruling.

Dred Scott was an enslaved man in the slave State of Missouri. His master took Scott, his wife Harriet, and their two daughters Eliza and Lizzie, and traveled with their master to the Free State of Illinois and the Free territory of Wisconsin, where Slavery was illegal, staying there four years. Later, when the master returned to Missouri with Scott's family, Scott filed a petition for his family's freedom, based on the fact that they had become legally free when they entered a free territory and State. Dred Scott filed first in Missouri State Court, then after losing, filed in US Federal Court. The case was then appealed to the Supreme Court of the United States of America. If the Court got it right, the whole entire population of enslaved people would be free. But that is not what happened. President-Elect James Buchanan, who during his election carried every slave State except Maryland and defeated anti-slavery Candidate John C. Fremont, said during his Inaugurational address that the Supreme Court's decision would permanently settle the issue of Slavery. President Buchanan also made it known he was in favor of a Federal Fugitive Slave Law, allowing slave owners to enter Free States and Territories to go after runaway persons of Color. The Court decision was rendered two days after the inauguration on March 6, 1857, stating that people of Color were not citizens and had no rights. The Supreme Court chose not to administer Equality.

The Scotts were soon after sold to a new owner, who manumitted Scott and his family on May 26, 1857. Scott later died in St. Louis, Missouri on September 17, 1858. His wife Harriet Robinson Scott lived on until June 1876. Lizzie lived on until 1945. Her sister Eliza went on to raise a family. There are living descendants of Dred and Harriet Scott today.

Lincoln was facing a growing fear that if he won the election the southern States would secede from the Union. And that is what they did upon Lincoln's election win on November 6, 1860. The Southern States had no plans of ever eliminating Slavery in their America. Instead, they simply created their own vision of Plantation America. But Lincoln – despite whether some say he didn't really intend to abolish slavery – issued an Executive Order, which emancipated millions. And millions of their living descendants today are documenting those ancestors, and the stories they passed down to their families.

Yet, the years 2020 and 2021 showcased to the world that the issues confronting Lincoln are still alive and well today. The year of George Floyd & Covid-19, and the year of the *Insurrection*. Those who lived through it will never forget it. Many are still living it. Where will the world find itself in 2045 – when the United Nations Organization celebrates its one hundredth anniversary? Or where will we be in 2026 – which marks the 400th anniversary of the African Arrival to New York? Pick any anniversary that looms in our future and ask when it arrives: Will *we*?

Attempting to document the ancestry of the world is a complicated study. Some things are now known, but many things still yet remain unknown. It is the author's belief that there were three brothers – the sons of Noah – who survived a catastrophic worldwide storm, and their wives in time would bear many children, who would become the nations of the world. In this essay, we have presented many things – the history of Kemet – the continent called Libya – the evidence of a land called Cush near Armenia – the existence of four rivers – the ancestors and descendants of Asia – the legends of a global flood. We have examined the origins of the Berbers and Carthage – the tribes of Europe – the empires of Greece and Rome – the East African Slave Trade – the enslaving of the Americas, Haiti and the Caribbean and those of African descent and Indigenous in New York, Virginia, and the Carolinas – the alliances between Christendom and the world powers. And finally, the issues facing the human family right now, including the issues of race, which is only a social construct (see Sources, Chapter Eleven/Race). There is only the human race, and many varieties therein. We are all genealogically related to one another, from three brothers. Can we not embrace and dignify one another? Can we not break bread together? We know all too well that a hearty meal or a feast brings people together. Just think of the international cuisine of the human family that all of us can enjoy something from: Italian lasagna and garlic bread; *Galumptkis*, also known as Russian cabbage rolls; Kalbi, or Korean beef short ribs; Japanese Sukiyaki, Shabu Shabu, and Yakitori; New Zealand's Colonial goose; Norway's lamb *Farikal*; German brathurst, wieners, *Rouladen*; a glass of French Riesling, Pinot blanc, or red Merlot; Swiss dessert, Greek and Turkish baklava, a piece of Irish soda bread; Vietnamese *pho*, Chinese Happy Family; India chicken curry and *tandoori roti*; Ethiopian *siga-wot* of berbere beef and injera; Southern barbeque pork ribs, greens, potato salad, peach cobbler; Cabernet Sauvignons from South Africa.

Chief Joseph also said: "We were taught to believe that the Great Spirit sees and hears everything, and that he never forgets." Daniel, the prophetic dream interpreter, also gave the credit to God. Besides having a dream about a little horn that would rise to be great, as the story goes, Daniel had another dream about the horn, and interpreted Nebuchadnezzar's nightmare about human governments:

*"I kept watching at that time because of the sound of the arrogant words that the horn was speaking; I watched until the beast was killed...but as for the rest of the beasts, their rulerships were taken away...the head of that image was of fine gold, its chest and its arms were of silver, its abdomen and its thighs were of copper, its legs were of iron, and its feet were partly of iron and partly of clay, You looked on until a stone was cut out, not by hands, and it struck the image on its feet of iron and of clay and crushed them...But the stone that struck the image became a large mountain, and it filled the whole earth."*

According to this ancient prophecy from Book 22 of the *Hagiographa* Writings, that nightmarish dream was a statue of a man, each part of his body corresponding to different metals – gold, silver, copper, iron – except for the feet, which comprised a mixture of iron and clay. Obviously, the weakest link of the statue image was in the feet, as iron and clay do not mix. To add more drama and intrigue, the old man Daniel foresaw a mysterious stone hurling toward the weakened feet, pulverizing the statue, then filling the whole earth. Emperors, Kings, Queens, and Presidents have all had their share of dreams. But could this one really hold meaning to our day? An African proverb says *"Even the best dancer on the stage must retire sometime."* Another proverb, from Ethiopia, says: *"What is inflated too much will break into fragments."*

On June 28, 1914, the heir to the Austria-Hungary throne, Archduke Franz Ferdinand was assassinated. Within weeks, the world had started the Great War. This was 2,520 years from the year when Wise man Daniel was taken prisoner to Babylon in 607 BCE. And since 1914 – the time of a *World* War – the world continues to fragment. Oppression and modern day Slavery continues to mount.

Will the descendants of Shem, Ham, and Japheth be able to resolve the issues facing them? Will the national groups of the Earth be able to live together in peace, or face annihilation in its future?

The alternative is a *Stone*, not made with hands, that is heading straight toward broken human rulership. Many may disagree with this appraisement. But therein lies the *Stone*, which appears to be our only hope.

# Acknowledgements

THERE WERE SEVERAL PEOPLE IN my life whom I've thanked over the years for inspiring me to write. Most of them have now passed and gone, including my parents, whom I think about constantly. But there are a few from the older generation who are still here. Thank you Laverne Brown, who is ninety, and was a dear friend to my parents. Her family story is retold on the *Portland Pioneers of Color Walking Tour*, when her parents' home was burned down twice for moving into a white neighborhood during the 1930's. Thank you Geraldine Daskalos, who is ninety-nine, and will turn one-hundred this year. Her daughter, my wife, I thank you for everything.

And there is Aunt Libby and Uncle Jim, who first met my mother and my maternal grandparents in 1950 at a fraternity called Friendship House in Portland, Oregon. Aunt Libby became my mother's maid of honor at my parents' wedding in 1957. Thank you Aunt Libby and Uncle Jim, for all the interesting books you gave me during my childhood and recently. I'm still enjoying the book Aunt Libby wrote – *The Nitty Gritty of Pottery Work* (2018).

Although my grandfather James Shelton passed on many years ago, he is still alive in my memory. I recall the day I interviewed him in 1989 when I first became interested in Genealogy, and he shared his oral family history: My grandfather on my mother's side was Lee Butler, and my grandfather on my dad's side was Richard Shelton, he was from Chattanooga…passed before I was born…my mother was Elter Butler, had some Indian in her, she was born in Dewitt, Arkansas and died when she was only 22…John Wesley Shelton was my dad, born in Tennessee."

I also thank Darlene Swanson and Van-Garde Imagery for such a super great job on the book design. There are so many more people I could thank in this section. One more person is Betty Hendricks, although she has also passed on. Betty was one of Jehovah's Witnesses. When she came to my next-door neighbor's home in 1974, I heard the stories she shared about her growing up during the Spanish flu in 1918 and World War I. My interest in history and biblical chronology was born from listening to those conversations.

During the early part of the year 2020, I found myself thinking about Betty and her description of the world during the Spanish Influenza, as the Covid-19 pandemic was preparing to deliver national devastation. As the year 2020 progressed, I saw more devastation, as the pandemic, police shootings of unarmed citizens, and worldwide demonstrations broke out. And then the year 2021 rolled around. On January 6th, the country saw on national TV an insurrection attempt in Washington D.C., followed by an impeachment, and a trial that just now concluded in acquittal. Where is this country headed for the future? Where is the international world heading? The distribution of the Vaccine continues, as the *haves* and the *have nots* dash to get in line. I will reserve my thoughts during this Black History Month, except to ask: Can things get any worse? If I could ask Betty that question right now, I know what she would tell me. She would pull out that well-used green cover Bible she carried with her, and would turn to the twenty-fourth chapter of Matthew and begin reading, putting emphasis on verses 14 and 21. Then she would turn to the Book of

Daniel and read about a large Stone heading our way.

If I'm still around by 2026, I'll ask myself that question again: Can things get any worse? Thank God there's a day coming when none of us will ever have to ask that question again.

February 13, 2021

# Sources

## CHAPTER TWO – The Sons of Japheth and Shem

*Transcaucasia at the End of the Early Bronze Age*, by Christoper Edens, Bulletin of the American Schools of Oriental Research, 299/300

Mountains of Ararat – https://en.wikipedia.org/Mountains_of_Ararat

The Holy Bible, King James Version Reference Bible; Published by Zondervan Publishing House, 1994

Genesis 11:2: "As they journeyed *from the east*." Footnote: "or, *eastward*"

*When Did Africans Get To Soviet Union?* (Part – 1), by Slava Tynes, The Afro-American, February 3, 1973. https://abkhazworld.com/aw/publications/archives/971

*Many Africans Came To The Soviet Union During Turkish Rule* (Part – 2), by Slava Tynes, *The Afro-American*, February 10, 1973. https://abkhazworld.com/aw/publications/archives/971

Third Servile War, also called The War of Spartacus https://en.wikipedia.org/Third_Servile_War

*Antiquities of the Jews*, Book XX, Chapter 9, and Book XVIII, Chapter 5, by Flavius Josephus (1st Century CE)

*Annals*, Book 15, Chapter 44, by Tacitus (116 CE)

Insight On The Scriptures, Vol. 1, Vol. 2, Watchtower Bible and Tract Society of New York, Inc. (1988)

CHAPTER THREE – The Sons of Ham

*Aegyptiaca (History of Egypt)* by Manetho, 3 Volumes. Verbrugghe, Gerald P.; Wickersham, John Moore (2001). Berossos and Manetho, Introduced and Translated: Native Traditions in Ancient Mesopotamia and Egypt.

*Thesaurus Geographicus*, by Abraham Ortelius, 1596 (First edition published 1570).

"Rejoined continents [This Dynamic Earth, USGS]" (http://pubs.usgs.gov/gip/dynamic/continents.html)

*Aboriginal Abkhazians of Russia – African Roots of Abkhazia*, Africasource.com, April 4, 2015 *Genetic evidence for an origin of the Armenians from Bronze Age mixing of multiple populations*, European Journal of Human Genetics, volume 24, pages 931 – 936 (2016) Published October 21, 2015

Nome (Egypt) – https://en.wikipedia.org/wiki/Nome_(Egypt)

*The Berbers (The Peoples of Africa)* Michael Brett, Elizabeth Fentress (1997)

*A History of the Maghrib*, by Jamil Abun-Nasr (1971)

*The Wars with Carthage*, by Chris Scarre, The Penguin Historical Atlas of Ancient Rome (1995)


CHAPTER FOUR – When Did Africa and China Make First Contact?

*The Importation Of Negro Slaves To China Under The Tang Dynasty* (A.D. 618-901), by Professor Chang Hsing-lang, Catholic University of Peking, Bulletin No. 7, December 1930, pages 37-59

*The Magical Kunlun and "Devil Slaves": Chinese Perceptions of Dark-skinned People and Africa before 1500*, by Julie Wilensky, Sino-Platonic Papers, Number 122, July 2002; Department of East Asian Languages and Civilizations, University of Pennsylvania

Lofton, R. (2015, March 09) *Africans And African Americans In China: A Long History, A Troubled Present, And A Promising Future?* https://www.blackpast.org

*Pan-Africanism in modern times: Challenges, concerns, and constraints* (2016), edited by Olayiwola Abegunrin and Sabella Ogbobode Abidde; p. 158

*Intimate Exclusion: Race and Caste Turned Inside Out*, by Martin Schoenhals (2003) page 26

*The Languages of China*, by S. Robert Ramsey (1987), page 253

*The Ho-ling Kuo Tiao*, Book 22, in *Hsin Tang Shu* (New History of Tang), edited by Ouyang Xiu and Song Qi (1060 CE),

*The Lin-yi Kuo Chuan*, Book 197, in *Chiu Tang Shu* (Old History of Tang), 10th Century CE

Chen-la Kuo, Book 10, and Book 222, Part II, in Hsin Tang Shu (New History of Tang)

*Wang Wu Tien Chu Kuo Chuan*, by Hui Ch'ao (8th Century CE)

*Chu Fan Chih,* by Chau Ju-K'uo (13th Century CE)

*Book of Jin*, edited by Fang Xuanling (648 CE)

*Beijing Apes Are Not Chinese Ancestors*, China News Net, January 14, 2005 http://www.sina.com.cn

*Narrative of the Third Voyage of Columbus as Contained in Las Casas's History* (Document No. AJ-066), American Journeys Collection, Digital Library And Archives, Wisconsin Historical Society; www.americanjourneys.org, www.wisconsinhistory.com

*Journals & Other Documents on the Life & Voyages of Christopher Columbus*, by Samuel Eliot Morison (1963)

*Esteban: The African Slave Who Explored America*, by Dennis Herrick (2018)

*They Came Before Columbus*, by Ivan Van Sertima (1976)

*The Early Peoples of Pre-Columbian America: Ivan Van Sertima and His Critics*, by Aaron K. Kamugisha, The Journal of Caribbean History_(/library/ p439833/the-journal-of-cribbean-history)


**CHAPTER FIVE – The East African Slave Trade and White Slavery**
Zanj – https://en.wikipedia.org/wiki/Zanj

*The Slave Trade in Eastern Africa*, by Rex Collins (1972)

*Christian Slaves, Muslim Masters: White Slavery in the Mediterranean, the Barbary Coast and Italy, 1500-1800*, by Robert C. Davis (2003)

*The Periplus Of The Erythraean Sea – Travel And Trade In The Indian Ocean By A Merchant Of The First Century*; Translated From The Greek and Annotated by Wilfred H. Schoff, a.m. (1912)


**CHAPTER SIX – Ancestry of the Caribbean, Haiti, and The Americas**
*Ancient Skeleton In Mexico Sheds Light On Americas Settlement,* by Scott Neuman, *All Things Considered*, NPR

*Migration Story*, the Chickasaw Nation, https://chickaswa.net/Our-Nation/ History/Prehistoric.aspxAncient

*DNA Reveals Complex Story of Human Migration Between Siberia and North America*, by Brian Handwerk, https://www.smithsonianmag.com/science-nature/ancient-dna-reveals-complex-story-human-migration

Haplogroup R1 – https://en.wikipedia.org/wiki/Haplogroup_R1

Wood, Karenne (editor). Virginia Indian Heritage Trail
www.chickahominytribe.org
encyclopediavirginia.org/entries/Chickahominy-tribe

## CHAPTER SEVEN – Enslavement of the Caribbean, Haiti, and The Americas

*Entwined Thread of Red and Black: The Hidden History of Indigenous Enslavement in Louisiana, 1699 – 1824*, A Thesis, by Leila K. Blackbird, B.A. University of New Orleans, 2017; December 2018

*The Legacy of African Slavery in Colonial Mexico, 1519 – 1810*, by Douglas Richmond, The Journal of Popular Culture / Volume 35, Issue 2, 05 March 2004

Opinion, *Slavery took hold in Florida under the Spanish in the 'forgotten century' of 1492 – 1619*, by J. Michael Francis, Gary Mormino, and Rachel Sanderson, *Tampa Bay Times*, August 29, 2019

*The Taíno were written off as extinct. Until now.* Newsweek.com. 20 February 2018, by Katherine Hignett

*What Became of the Taíno*, by Robert M. Poole, Smithsonian Magazine (October 2011)

*The Legend of Hatuey, The History of Cuba*, by J.A. Sierra (August 2006).

*Bartolomé de Las Casas, Short Account of the Destruction of the Indies.* Translated by Nigel Griffin. (London: Penguin, 1999)

*African Heritage and Memories of Slavery in Brazil and the South Atlantic World*, by Ana Araujo (2015)

*The Aftershocks of History*, by L. Dubois (2012)

*The Slaves who Defeated Napoléon: Toussaint L'Ouverture and the Haitian War of Independence, 1801–1804*, by Philippe Girard (2011)

*Pope Nicolas V and the Portuguese Slave Trade*, African Laborers for a New Empire: Iberia, Slavery, and the Atlantic World, https://ldhi.library.cofc.edu/exhibits/show/african_laborers_or_a_new_emp/pope_nicolas_v_and_the_portugese_slave_trade

*Portuguese Colonialism And Japanese Slaves*, by Michio Kitahara (2013)

https://asiaone.com/News, *Japanese slaves taken to Mexico in 16th century*, The Yomiuri Shimbun/Asia News Network, May 14, 2013


## CHAPTER EIGHT - 1626

*New York City's Slave Market*, by Sylviane Diouf, New York Public Library (2015)

Newnetherlandinstitute.org/Slavery in New Netherland

*The Freedmen of New Amsterdam*, by Peter R. Christoph, Selected Rensselaerswijck Seminar Papers, A Beautiful And Fruitful Place, Volume 1 (1991) New York State Library

*Slave Market*, Mapping the AfricanAmerican Past https://maap.columbia.edu/place/22.html

The Project Gutenberg eBook, Journal of Jasper Danckaerts, 1679 – 1680, by Jasper Danckaerts, Edited by Barlett Burleigh James and J. Franklin Jameson, Translated by Henry C. Murphy

*Slavery in New York*, by New York Historical Society


## CHAPTER NINE – Enslavement of Indigenous and Africans in Virginia and the Carolinas

*Indian Slavery In Colonial Virginia And South Carolina*, A Thesis, by Kevin J. Bertelsen (1984)

North Carolina American Indian History Timeline / NC Museum of History https://www.ncmuseumofhistory.org/american-indian/handouts/timeline

Letter From Secretary of the Interior, 1914, Report on the Condition and Tribal Rights of Robeson and Adjoining Counties of North Carolina, June 30, 1914

Tuscarora War – https://en.wikipedia.org/wiki/Tuscarora_War

ESKRIDGE

Westmoreland County, Virginia

Orphan Distributions, Reel 32, Page 3, Samuel Eskridge, Decd, 1756

Richard Edmund Eskridge of Edgefield County, South Carolina was born about 1775. After his wife Nancy Livingston Eskridge died in 1821, R. Eskridge moved to Alabama. His brother Austin Pollard Eskridge, born 1779, also headed there, settling in Marengo County, Alabama. A former French colony once existed there, due to a number of French refugees who fled Haiti during the Haitian slavery Revolution. Austin Pollard's son was Richard Madison Eskridge, who in 1850 held seventeen enslaved persons in Marengo County. By 1860, Richard Madison Eskridge had moved to Clarke County, Mississippi. After the Civil war, the 1870 census of Mississippi lists an African American couple, Zachariah and Rachel Eskridge, living in Jasper County, MS, not far from Clarke County. The family is listed living next door to Native indigenous families surnamed Gandy and Johnston. Zachariah and Rachel had several children, including Sydney Eskridge, born about 1874. In 1900, an African American couple named David and Louisa Eskridge were living in Jasper County. The couple had gotten married in Clarke County in 1889. On the 1910 census for Lincoln County, MS in an area of the town called Brookhaven, there is listed two families, one headed by a male "S.D. Eskridge," and the other "Henry Eskridge." Both listed as African American. North Carolina Probate Records, 1735 – 1970, Caswell County, Record of Wills, Inventories & Settlements Of Estates, Book G, Page 124, Richard Eskridge, 1816

North Carolina Probate Records, 1735 – 1970, Rutherford County Record of Wills 1823 - 1833, Richard Eskridge, 1832

In the last will and testament of Richard Eskridge of Rutherford County, NC, he bequeathed two enslaved girls to his son John Eskridge: "I give and bequeath unto my son John Eskridge two Negro girls, one named ALHA and the other HESWILLY." John Eskridge later moved to Tennessee. On the 1830 census, he is listed in Lincoln County with two enslaved females, born between 1794 – 1810. On the 1850 census, John Eskridge is listed in

Winchester, Franklin County with an enslaved female born about 1801, with her enslaved family.

North Carolina Freedmen's Bureau, Assistant Commissioner Records 1862 – 1870, Register of letters received, Vol 2 (3), Nov. 1866 – Feb. 1868

The Freedmen's Bureau Online, https://freedmensbureau.com/northcarolina/northcarolinaoutrages2.htm

## CHAPTER TEN – Religion's Involvement in the Slave Trade
*Pope Nicolas V and the Portuguese Slave Trade*, African Laborers for a New Empire: Iberia, Slavery, and the Atlantic World, https://ldhi.library.cofc.edu/exhibits/show/african_laborers_or_a_new_emp/pope_nicolas_v_and_the_portugese_slave_trade

Zulu royal family – htts://en.wikipedia.org/wiki/Zulu_royal_family

## CHAPTER ELEVEN – The World's Ancestry – Our Future?
### Race a Social Construct
"A race is simply on of the partially isolated gene pools into which the human species came to be divided during and following its early geographical spread… Roughly one race has developed on each of the five major continental areas of the earth. As we would expect, divergence appears to be correlated with the degree of isolation."
*Heredity and Human Life*, by Hamilton L. Carson (1963)

"When they study racial differences, scientists investigate the way by which particular traits are passed on from parents to children…The scientist realizes that every time he measures intelligence in any man, black or white, his results show the intelligence that man was born with *plus* what happened to him since he was born….The differences did not arise because people were from the North or the South, or because they were white or black, but because of difference in income, education, cultural advantages and other opportunities."

*The Races of Mankind*, by Professor Ruth Benedict and Dr. Gene Weltfish (1956)

**Human skin color** ranges from the darkest brown to the lightest hues. Differences in skin color among individuals is caused by variation in pigmentation, which is the result of genetics (inherited from one's biological parents…Melanin is produced by cells called melanocytes in a process called melanogenesis… People have different skin colors mainly because their melanocytes produce different amount and kinds of melanin.
*En.wikipedia.org/wiki/Human_skin_color*

So we see that early in human history, when a group of people were isolated from the rest of mankind and married within their own group, certain distinctive combinations of genetic traits were emphasized in their offspring.

# Photo Credits

Front Cover Photo: Giant ocean wave.jpg;
(https://creativecommons.org/publicdomain/zero/1.0/deed.en)

Great Sphinx of Giza and the Pyramid of Khafre
Author: Most likely Hamish2k; (GFDL, CC By_SA 3.0)
Commons.wikimedia.org/wiki/File:Egypt.Giza.Sphinx.02.jpg

Map of Armenia
Author: Semhur (Wikimedia Commons / CC By-SA-3.0)

A Black Family from Adzyubzha, Public Domain

Tunis Bab Souika 1899, Public Domian

Gondola on the Grand Canal
Author:Peter K. Burian (CC By-SA 4.0)
Commons.wikimedia.org/wiki/File:Gondola_on_the_Grand_Canal_
Venice_Italy.jpg

Greek Man
Author: Wolfgang Sauber; (GFDL, CC By-SA 1.2)
Commons.wikimedia.org/wiki/File:Vamos_-_Kafenion_3.jpg

19th Century reconstruction of Eratosthenes' map of the known world, c.
194 BC
Commons.wikimedia.org/wiki/File:Mappa_di_Eratostene.jpg

Tripoli, Libya
Author: Abdul-Jawad Elhusuni; (CC By-SA 3.0)
Commons.wikimedia.org/wiki/File:Tripoli_Central_Business_District_Oea_Park.jpg

Chinese Family, 1869, Public Domain
Author: John Thompson; Welcome Collection, London

Manchu Ladies at a Meal Table, 1869; Public Domain
Author: John Thompson; Welcome Collection, London

Native Americans Today
Author: Robfergusonjr (GFDL, 1.2
Commons.wikimedia.org/wiki/File:Native_Americans_Today.jpg

Olmec Heads; Public Domain

Harlem, NY, 1925
Public Domain (CC By-SA 4.0)

The Congo (author MONUSCO photos
https://commons.wikimedia.org/wiki/File:Photo_of_the_Day_17_February_2014_(12589890963).jpg

Chief Joseph and Family, c. 1880; Public Domain; Washington State History Museum

Two Women on Eskridge Plantation, 1850's
Author: Will Minter; with permission

Hausa women, 30 October 2007
Author: prettydougla; (https://creativecommons.org/licenses/by/2.0/deed.en)

Palestinian women
Author: TheElders
Photo credit: Haim Zach (CC By 2.0)
Commons.wikimedia.org/wiki/File:ela_Bhatt_meets_youg_Palestinian_women_in_Ramallah.jpg

Mahane Yehuda Market P1020256.jpg
Author: deror_avi
GNU Free Documentation
Commons.wikimedia.org/wiki/File:Mahane_Yehuda_Market_P1020256.jpg

Black Hebrews Dimona children.jpg
Author: Dror Eiger
(https://creativecommons.org/licenses/by-sa/2.0/deed.en)

www.ingramcontent.com/pod-product-compliance
Lightning Source LLC
Chambersburg PA
CBHW041214030426
42336CB00023B/3348